Credits

Author

Shi Chuan

Reviewers

Dale Cruse

Sarah Soward

Shawn McBurnie

Acquisition Editor

Alina Lewis

Lead Technical Editor

Shreerang Deshpande

Technical Editor

Sakina Kaydawala

Project Coordinator

Leena Purkait

Proofreader

Bernadette Watkins

Indexer

Monica Ajmera Mehta

Production Coordinator

Prachali Bhiwandkar

Cover Work

Prachali Bhiwandkar

About the Author

Shi Chuan has over five years experience in web development. He is a member of the HTML5 Boilerplate project, lead developer of Mobile Boilerplate (`http://h5bp.com/mobile`), owner of the JavaScript Patterns project (`http://shichuan.github.com/javascript-patterns`). He is now an independent developer living in the UK and China. You can find out more about him on his personal website at: `http://www.blog.highub.com`. He loves reading, travelling, great food, and eclectic and indie music.

I would like to thank my parents, and the whole family who have been my positive and unconditional supporters. I would also like to thank Jiang Xue, who taught me so many things about life, in ways she does not even know.

I would also like to thank my friends from the Boilerplate Team - Paul Irish, Divya Manian, Mathias Bynens, and Nicolas Gallagher. Former CTO of the company I worked for - Chi Tran. They have been and will always be my inspiration and aspiration.

HTML5 Mobile Development Cookbook

Over 60 recipes for building fast, responsive HTML5 mobile websites for iPhone 5, Android, Windows Phone, and Blackberry

Shi Chuan

PUBLISHING

BIRMINGHAM - MUMBAI

HTML5 Mobile Development Cookbook

First published: February, 2012

Production Reference: 1240112

Published by Packt Publishing Ltd.
Livery Place
35 Livery Street
Birmingham B3 2PB, UK.

ISBN 978-1-84969-196-3

www.packtpub.com

Cover Image by Rakesh Shejwal (shejwal.rakesh@gmail.com)

About the Reviewers

Dale Cruse, a Boston-area web developer, is the author of *HTML5 Multimedia Development Cookbook*. He has been publishing websites for high-profile clients ranging from the U.S. Army to Bloomingdale's since 1995. He has been a guest lecturer at the Art Institute of New England and is currently pursuing speaking opportunities. Contact him at `http://dalejcruse.com`. He is also the author of the Champagne blog *Drinks Are On Me* at `http://drinksareonme.net`.

Sarah Soward teaches coding, design, and the Adobe Creative suite at the Bay Area Video Coalition and AcademyX. In addition to teaching, she also developed the curriculum for BAVC's HTML5/CSS3, Color Theory, Typography, Fireworks, and Web Design Workflow classes. For a number of years, she was the Art Director of non-profits. She is the co-author of the *WordPress and Flash Cookbook*. When she isn't teaching, she's designing and developing everything from business cards to websites, painting rhinos, building stuff, and banging on a drum till her hands keep their own beat. She likes to keep busy.

www.PacktPub.com

Support files, eBooks, discount offers and more

You might want to visit www.PacktPub.com for support files and downloads related to your book.

Did you know that Packt offers eBook versions of every book published, with PDF and ePub files available? You can upgrade to the eBook version at www.PacktPub.com and as a print book customer, you are entitled to a discount on the eBook copy. Get in touch with us at service@packtpub.com for more details.

At www.PacktPub.com, you can also read a collection of free technical articles, sign up for a range of free newsletters and receive exclusive discounts and offers on Packt books and eBooks.

http://PacktLib.PacktPub.com

Do you need instant solutions to your IT questions? PacktLib is Packt's online digital book library. Here, you can access, read and search across Packt's entire library of books.

Why Subscribe?

- Fully searchable across every book published by Packt
- Copy and paste, print and bookmark content
- On demand and accessible via web browser

Free Access for Packt account holders

If you have an account with Packt at www.PacktPub.com, you can use this to access PacktLib today and view nine entirely free books. Simply use your login credentials for immediate access.

For Claire Jiang Xue

Table of Contents

Preface

How do I create fast and responsive mobile websites that work across a range of platforms? For developers dealing with the proliferation of mobile devices each with unique screen sizes and performance limitations, it is an important question. This cookbook provides the answer. You will learn how to apply the latest HTML5 mobile web features effectively across a range of mobile devices.

HTML5 Mobile Development Cookbook will show you how to plan, build, debug, and optimize mobile websites. Apply the latest HTML5 features that are best for mobile, while discovering emerging mobile web features to integrate in your mobile sites.

Build a rock-solid default mobile HTML template and understand mobile user interaction. Make your site fast and responsive, leveraging the uniqueness of location-based mobile features and mobile rich media. Make your mobile website perfect using debugging, performance optimization, and server-side tuning. The book finishes with a sneak preview of future mobile web technologies.

What this book covers

Chapter 1, HTML5 and the Mobile Web, introduces HTML5 and the mobile web, along with some emulators and simulators.

Chapter 2, Mobile Setup and Optimization, discusses various mobile setups and optimization, such as preventing text resize and optimizing viewport width.

Chapter 3, Interactive Media with Mobile Events, discusses mobile interactions such as gesture events.

Chapter 4, Building Fast and Responsive Websites, talks about the various ways to make mobile websites fast and responsive.

Chapter 5, Mobile Device Access, discusses location-based mobile web and other HTML5 device-specific features.

Chapter 6, Mobile Rich Media, talks about the HTML5 rich media elements that can be used on mobile browsers.

Chapter 7, Mobile Debugging, teaches you ways to work around mobile screen-side constraints and debug mobile websites and web apps effectively.

Chapter 8, Server-Side Tuning, focuses on the server-side tuning for mobile websites.

Chapter 9, Mobile Performance Testing, teaches you various Tools and techniques that can be used to boost mobile performance.

Chapter 10, Emerging Mobile Web Features, talks about ECMAScript 5 as well as mobile-specific features that were added to allow more functionalities with mobile and boost the performance.

What you need for this book

A text editor is all that is needed for most recipes in the book. You should also have a mobile device such as an iPhone, Android, Blackberry, or other device suitable for testing. Although it is best to test things out on a real device, don't worry if you don't have one, because we will cover details on how to use emulators and simulators to test, in case a real device is not available.

Who this book is for

Developers keen to create HTML5 mobile websites that are fast and responsive across a whole range of mobile devices.

Conventions

In this book, you will find a number of styles of text that distinguish between different kinds of information. Here are some examples of these styles, and an explanation of their meaning.

Code words in text are shown as follows: "geolocation is a new property on the navigator object."

A block of code is set as follows:

```
var latitude = position.coords.latitude;
var longitude = position.coords.longitude;
var accuracy = position.coords.accuracy;
```

When we wish to draw your attention to a particular part of a code block, the relevant lines or items are set in bold:

```
var latitude = position.coords.latitude;
var longitude = position.coords.longitude;
var accuracy = position.coords.accuracy;
```

New terms and **important words** are shown in bold. Words that you see on the screen, in menus or dialog boxes for example, appear in the text like this: "Click on the **Start** button in the **Capture Options** dialog to start capturing."

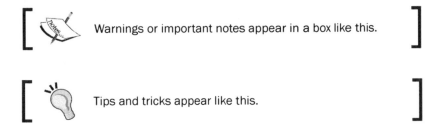

Warnings or important notes appear in a box like this.

Tips and tricks appear like this.

Reader feedback

Feedback from our readers is always welcome. Let us know what you think about this book—what you liked or may have disliked. Reader feedback is important for us to develop titles that you really get the most out of.

To send us general feedback, simply send an e-mail to feedback@packtpub.com, and mention the book title via the subject of your message.

If there is a book that you need and would like to see us publish, please send us a note in the **SUGGEST A TITLE** form on www.packtpub.com or e-mail suggest@packtpub.com.

If there is a topic that you have expertise in and you are interested in either writing or contributing to a book, see our author guide on www.packtpub.com/authors.

Customer support

Now that you are the proud owner of a Packt book, we have a number of things to help you to get the most from your purchase.

Downloading the example code for this book

You can download the example code files for all Packt books you have purchased from your account at `http://www.PacktPub.com`. If you purchased this book elsewhere, you can visit `http://www.PacktPub.com/support` and register to have the files e-mailed directly to you.

Errata

Although we have taken every care to ensure the accuracy of our content, mistakes do happen. If you find a mistake in one of our books—maybe a mistake in the text or the code—we would be grateful if you would report this to us. By doing so, you can save other readers from frustration and help us improve subsequent versions of this book. If you find any errata, please report them by visiting `http://www.packtpub.com/support`, selecting your book, clicking on the **errata submission form** link, and entering the details of your errata. Once your errata are verified, your submission will be accepted and the errata will be uploaded on our website, or added to any list of existing errata, under the Errata section of that title. Any existing errata can be viewed by selecting your title from `http://www.packtpub.com/support`.

Piracy

Piracy of copyright material on the Internet is an ongoing problem across all media. At Packt, we take the protection of our copyright and licenses very seriously. If you come across any illegal copies of our works, in any form, on the Internet, please provide us with the location address or website name immediately so that we can pursue a remedy.

Please contact us at `copyright@packtpub.com` with a link to the suspected pirated material.

We appreciate your help in protecting our authors, and our ability to bring you valuable content.

Questions

You can contact us at `questions@packtpub.com` if you are having a problem with any aspect of the book, and we will do our best to address it.

1

HTML5 and the Mobile Web

In this chapter, we will cover:

- ▶ Getting your mobile device ready
- ▶ Emulators and simulators
- ▶ Setting up the mobile development environment
- ▶ Using HTML5 on mobile web
- ▶ Making HTML5 render cross browser
- ▶ Designing for mobile
- ▶ Determining your target mobile devices
- ▶ Defining a content adaptation strategy

Introduction

Both HTML5 and mobile web are promising technologies. Both have relatively short histories. In this chapter, most topics we will be covering are relatively basic. This is to help you get started with mobile development quickly and with minimum effort.

Both mobile and HTML5 are still evolving in nature and there could be many questions in your mind. We will clear those doubts and set your mind focused on things that matter.

The mobile web is growing fast. We now have mobile Safari which is one of the most used apps on the iPhone, allowing developers to build high performance web applications and enhancing users' browsing experience. You do not need a developer account to host and run a mobile site, you don't need to get approval from any app market to launch a mobile website and you can make updates any time you like without the hassle of waiting for approval. All these are benefits of mobile web development, but at the same time, there are challenges such as inconsistencies among browsers, the lack of certain features compared to native apps, and security. We can't tackle them all, but we sure can solve some of them. And we will see, when developing a mobile site, how we can separate the common practices from the best practices.

There are literally thousands of smartphones out there; you don't need every single one of them to test your application on. In fact, you may need fewer than 10. If that's still out of your budget, then two devices are good enough. For the rest, you can use simulators/emulators to do the job. This book focuses on six A-grade mobile devices, with focus specifically on iPhone, Android, and Windows Phone:

- ► iOS
- ► Android
- ► Windows Mobile
- ► Blackberry v6.0 and above
- ► Symbian 60
- ► Palm webOS

There are two browsers that are device-independent that will also be covered in this book. They are:

- ► Opera Mobile
- ► Firefox Mobile

Just because other browsers are not in the list does not mean they won't be covered by the issues and techniques we discuss in this book.

Identifying your target mobile devices

Target browser: all

You can't possibly make a mobile site for every single mobile device. No one has the time or energy to do so.

Cross-browser mobile web development can be crazy. It's hard to define the scope of the work, as *John Resig* (creator of jQuery Mobile) pointed out in his presentation slide describing his experience building jQuery Mobile (`http://www.slideshare.net/jeresig/testing-mobile-javascript`), he asked three questions:

- ▶ Which platforms and browsers are popular?

- ▶ Which browsers are capable of supporting modern scripting?

- ▶ What devices and simulators do I acquire to test with?

When you are building a mobile site, you have to ask yourself similar questions, but not the exact same questions, because remember your site should be specifically tailored to your target audience. So your questions should be:

- ▶ Which platforms and browsers are most commonly used by visitors on my website?

- ▶ How many people access my website from a mobile device that is capable of supporting modern scripting?

- ▶ Which devices and simulators do I need for testing?

Which platforms and browsers are most commonly used by visitors on my website?

Now let's answer the first question. Before building a mobile website, you must first find out who are your target audience, and what mobile devices they use when visiting your site. There are many analytics tools that can help you answer these questions. One of those is Google Analytics. You can sign up for a free Google Analytics account at: `http://www.google.com/analytics/`

The way to do it is fairly straightforward: most developers are no strangers to Google Analytics. All you have to do is to include the JavaScript snippet from the the Google Analytics site and embed it in your web pages.

JavaScript can be rendered in most modern smartphones, so there is really no difference between using it on a desktop site and on a mobile site.

How many people access my website from a mobile device that is capable of supporting modern scripting?

Now let's answer the second question. One thing you may want to find out is the number of people using mobile browsers to surf your site. And you also want to find out how many people use a relic mobile browser that doesn't support JavaScript at all. This is because if the percentage of people using low-end smartphones is higher than that of people using high-end smartphones, it may not be worthwhile using HTML5 in the first place (although the chance of this is very low).

So if your goal is not just to know the number of people using smartphones, but also the number of people who use older versions of mobile phones, Google Analytics for mobile comes to the rescue. You can download the script from:

```
http://code.google.com/mobile/analytics/download.html#Download_the_
Google_Analytics_server_side_package
```

Google Analytics for mobile server-side packages currently supports JSP, ASPX, Perl, and PHP. Let's take a look at one of the examples in PHP. All you have to do is to change the **ACCOUNT ID GOES HERE** with your GA account ID. But remember to **replace 'UA-xx' with 'MO-xx'**.

Unfortunately, when you use the server-side version, you can't use it on pages where you also use the standard JavaScript tracking code, ga.js. Using the server-side version means that you have to give up the JavaScript version. It can be annoying because the JavaScript version provides a lot of dynamic tracking mechanisms that are lacking in the server-side version:

```php
<?php
  // Copyright 2009 Google Inc. All Rights Reserved.
  $GA_ACCOUNT = "ACCOUNT ID GOES HERE";
  $GA_PIXEL = "ga.php";

  function googleAnalyticsGetImageUrl() {
    global $GA_ACCOUNT, $GA_PIXEL;
    $url = "";
    $url .= $GA_PIXEL . "?";
    $url .= "utmac=" . $GA_ACCOUNT;
    $url .= "&utmn=" . rand(0, 0x7fffffff);

    $referer = $_SERVER["HTTP_REFERER"];
    $query = $_SERVER["QUERY_STRING"];
    $path = $_SERVER["REQUEST_URI"];

    if (empty($referer)) {
      $referer = "-";
    }
    $url .= "&utmr=" . urlencode($referer);

    if (!empty($path)) {
      $url .= "&utmp=" . urlencode($path);
    }

    $url .= "&guid=ON";

    return $url;
  }
?>
```

Alternatives to Google Analytics

Google Analytics is not the only mobile analytics service in the market. There are other services providing more specialized services. For example, **PercentMobile** is a hosted mobile analytics service that makes your mobile audience and opportunities clear. You can find out more about this service at:

```
http://percentmobile.com/
```

Accuracy of Google Analytics

The location reported by mobile devices may not always be accurate; Google Analytics uses IP addresses to determine user location for Map Overlay reports. They are subject to possible inaccuracy, as mobile IPs originate from the wireless carrier gateway which is not necessarily co-located with mobile users.

Server loading speed concern

Due to the server-side processing, some additional server load may be incurred. Google recommends you first test the snippet on a few of your pages to ensure all is well before rolling out to an entire site.

Setting up mobile development tools

Target browser: all

Now one question still remains unanswered from the previous recipe: *which devices and simulators do I need for testing?* We will find this out in this chapter.

If you have figured out what major mobile devices you are going to support, now is the time to see how to set them up. Mobile development can be costly if you test on various mobile devices. Although we have all these mobile simulators and emulators available for testing, it's not as good as testing on a real device. Now let's see how we can maximize the testing coverage and minimize the cost.

Getting ready

We are going to make some assumptions here. Each case is different, but the idea is the same. Let's assume you have a Windows operating system on your desktop, but the top visitors to your site surf using iOS, Android, and Blackberry.

How to do it...

Your goal is to maximize the coverage and minimize the cost. All three devices have emulators, but not all support different platforms.

Name	Compatibility
iOS simulator	Mac
Android emulator	Windows, Mac, Linux
Blackberry simulator	Windows

As you can see, since iOS simulator only works for Mac, and if you are running a Windows OS, the best and only choice is to purchase an iPhone for testing. For Android and Blackberry, because they both have emulators for Windows, to save budget, you can download the emulators.

How it works...

1. List the top mobile devices people use to surf your site.
2. Know the machine OS you are using for the development.
3. Find out the compatibility of each of these device emulators to your development environment.

There's more...

If you have the budget for more than one mobile device having a different OS, you can think further about screen sizes and the DPI of the mobile device. You may not need to buy two high-end devices. For instance, it's not necessary to own an iPhone4 and an Android Thunderbolt. You can buy a lower-end of Android just to test out how your site would look on a lower-end device. So the idea is to combine your OS, mobile devices, and emulators to maximize the scenarios to cover.

Device simulator/emulator download lookup table

The following table shows a list of popular mobile device emulators for mobile web design and development testing:

Name	Type	Compatibility	URL
iOS	Simulator	Mac	`https://developer.apple.com/devcenter/ios/index.action#downloads`
Android	Emulator	Mac, Win, Linux	`http://developer.android.com/sdk/index.html`

Name	Type	Compatibility	URL
HP webOS	Virtual Machine	Mac, Win, Linux	`http://developer.palm.com/index.php?option=com_content&view=article&id=1788&Itemid=55`
Nokia Symbian	Emulator	Win	`http://www.forum.nokia.com/info/sw.nokia.com/id/ec866fab-4b76-49f6-b5a5-af0631419e9c/S60_All_in_One_SDKs.html`
Blackberry	Emulator	Win	`http://us.blackberry.com/developers/resources/simulators.jsp`
Windows Mobile 7	Emulator	Win	`http://www.microsoft.com/downloads/en/details.aspx?FamilyID=04704acf-a63a-4f97-952c-8b51b34b00ce`

Browser simulator/emulator download lookup table

Apart from device testing tools, we also have tools for platform-independent browsers, notably Opera and Firefox. These are shown in the table below:

Name	Type	Compatibility	URL
Opera Mobile	Emulator	Mac, Win, Linux	`http://www.opera.com/developer/tools/`
Opera Mini	Simulator	Mac, Win, Linux	`http://www.opera.com/developer/tools/http://www.opera.com/mobile/demo/`
Firefox for Mobile	Simulator	Mac, Win, Linux	`http://www.mozilla.com/en-US/mobile/download/`

Remote testing

Apart from emulators and simulators, there are also test frameworks that give you remote access to REAL devices. One of those tools is **DeviceAnywhere**; one problem is that it is not free.

`http://www.deviceanywhere.com/`

BlackBerry simulator

Target Browser: BlackBerry

Most mobile device simulators are easy to install and configure if you follow the instructions on their sites, but BlackBerry simulators work differently from other mobile device simulators. For Blackberry device simulators, to connect to Internet, besides downloading the simulators, you also need to download and install **BlackBerry Email and MDS Services Simulator**.

Getting ready

Make sure you have chosen a simulator to download from: `http://us.blackberry.com/ developers/resources/simulators.jsp`

How to do it...

First, go to the page: `https://swdownloads.blackberry.com/Downloads/ entry.do?code=A8BAA56554F96369AB93E4F3BB068C22&CPID=OTC-SOFTWAREDOWNLOADS&cp=OTC-SOFTWAREDOWNLOADS`. There you will see a list of products similar to the following screenshot:

Now select **BlackBerry Email and MDS Services Simulator Package** and then click on **Next**.

After downloading and installing the software, you must first launch the service simulator before the Blackberry simulator, in order to allow it to connect to the Internet.

The following is a screenshot of a Blackberry simulator:

Setting up the mobile development environment

Target browser: all

Before we start mobile web development, we have to first set up a development environment.

Getting ready

1. Set up localhost on your machine. For Windows, Mac, or Linux, the easiest way to set it up is to use the popular and free XAMPP software: (http://www.apachefriends.org/en/index.html).

2. Make sure you have a wireless connection.

3. Also you should have a mobile device with you. Otherwise, use a mobile simulator/emulator.

4. Ensure your mobile device and your desktop are on the same wireless network.

How to do it...

1. Create an HTML file and name it `ch01e1.html` at the root directory of your localhost:

   Inside `ch01r01.html`, type in the following:

   ```
   <html>
     <head>
     <meta name="viewport" content="width=device-width, initial-
   scale=1.0">
     </head>
     <body>
       <header>
       Main Navigation here
       </header>
   body content here
       <footer>
       Footer links here
       </footer>
     </body>
   </html>
   ```

2. Now get your IP address. If you are using Windows, you can type the following line in your command prompt:

   ```
   ipconfig
   ```

Downloading the example code for this book

You can download the example code files for all Packt books you have purchased from your account at http://www.PacktPub.com. If you purchased this book elsewhere, you can visit http://www.PacktPub.com/support and register to have the files e-mailed directly to you

3. Once you have got your IP address, (for example, `192.168.1.16`.), enter it in your mobile browser URL address bar. Now you should see the page load with the text displayed:

How it works...

Within the same network, your mobile device can access your desktop host through your desktop IP address.

There's more...

If you don't have a mobile device, you can use one of the simulators for testing. But it's recommended to have at least one or two real mobile devices for testing. A simulator could test most things, but not everything, accurately.

Testing on a Safari desktop

If your main target audience is iPhone mobile Safari users, you can also do testing on a desktop to save time. To do so, open up Safari, go to **Preferences**, click on the **Advanced** tab, check **Show Develop menu bar** as shown next:

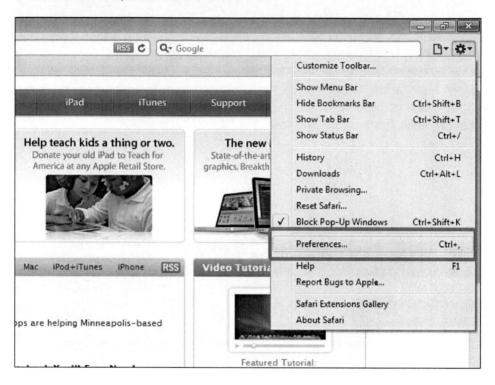

Now click on the display menu for the current page, choose **Develop | User Agent | Mobile Safari 3.1.3 – iPhone**:

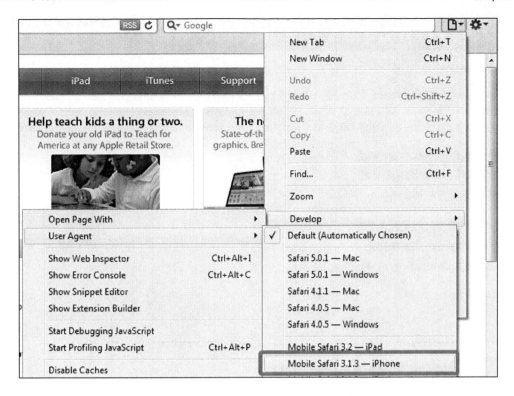

List of community-based collection of emulators/simulators

There is a list of emulators and simulators available if you really don't have a Smartphone at hand. You can find the list on a wiki on the Mobile Boilerplate project:

```
https://github.com/h5bp/mobile-boilerplate/wiki/Mobile-Emulators-&-
Simulators
```

List of emulators/simulators collection by Firtman

Maximiliano Firtman, a mobile and web developer, also an author, maintains a list of emulators on his site at:

```
http://www.mobilexweb.com/emulators
```

Using HTML5 on the mobile web

Target browser: all

Now we are going to create a simple HTML5 page for your mobile device. If you already have experience with older versions of HTML, HTML5 should be easy to understand. And if you have made a web page for desktop before, it won't be hard for you to make one for a mobile device.

Getting ready

Create a new file `ch01e2.html`.

How to do it...

Save the following code in the file:

```
<!doctype html>
<html>
  <head>
  <meta name="viewport" content="width=device-width, initial-
scale=1.0">
  </head>
  <body>
    hello to the HTML5 world!
  </body>
</html>
```

Now render this in your mobile browser, and you should see the text render just as expected.

How it works...

As you can see, the only difference between HTML5 and other HTML pages is the **Document Type Definition** (**DTD**) we used: `<!doctype html>`.

You might have seen the code `<meta name="viewport" content="width=device-width, initial-scale=1.0">` and are wondering what it does. It helps Mobile Safari to know that the page is as wide as the device. Setting `initial-scale=1` tells the browser not to zoom in or out.

There's more...

Here's a little bit of history of HTML5: there are two versions of HTML5 draft, one created by W3C and the other by WHATWG. The W3C is run by a group that is democratic in nature, but super slow in practice. WHATWG is edited by one person, *Ian Hickson* (who is also working for Google), and a group of people who are not public. As *Ian* does most of the decision making, it makes WHATWG's version progress faster.

HTML5 and version number

You might be wondering why HTML5 is being so ambiguous by using a declaration without even a version number. Well there are many reasons to justify this:

1. Version support of HTML doesn't matter much to browsers. What matters is the feature support. In other words, if the browser supports the HTML5 feature you are using, even if you declare the document as HTML4, it will still render the HTML5 element as expected.

2. It's easier to type!

Mobile doctypes

One question you may ask is whether it is safe to use the HTML5 DTD `<!doctype html>`. The answer is DTDs were made for validation, not browser rendering. Your next question might be: what about quirks mode? `<!doctype html>` is the minimum information required to ensure that a browser renders in standards mode. So you are pretty safe to use `<!doctype html>`.

You may have noticed that we use `<!doctype html>` instead of `<!DOCTYPE html>`. The reason is HTML5 is not case sensitive, but for consistency with other HTML tags, we will use lowercase throughout the book.

Free resources to learn HTML5

There are many excellent and free books, and articles about basic HTML5 tags. If you are unfamiliar with HTML5, you can check out one of the following:

- ▶ HTML5 Doctor: `http://html5doctor.com/`
- ▶ Dive Into HTML5: `http://diveintohtml5.org/`
- ▶ HTML5 Rocks: `http://www.html5rocks.com/`

If you are the kind of person who really wants to know every detail about something, you can read the official HTML5 specs.

The W3C version of the spec is at:

```
http://dev.w3.org/html5/spec/Overview.html
```

The WHATWG version of HTML Living Standard is at:

```
http://www.whatwg.org/specs/web-apps/current-work/multipage/
```

Rendering HTML5 across different browsers

Target browser: all

There are older mobile browsers that don't recognize HTML5 elements. The problem with this is that you can't style these elements if they are not recognized. There are many shims made to tackle this issue. One of those is Modernizr.

Getting ready

1. One of the mobile browsers that doesn't recognize HTML5 elements is Windows Mobile. If you don't have Windows Mobile, you can simply use IE7 to test this out, because they are based on the same engine.

2. Download Modernizr from the site: `http://www.modernizr.com/`. It was written by *Faruk Ateş*, *Paul Irish*, and *Alex Sexton*.

How to do it...

1. Create an HTML file and name it `ch01e3.html`, and enter the following code in the file:

```
<!doctype html>
<html>
  <head>
  <meta charset="utf-8">
  <meta name="viewport" content="width=device-width,
initial-scale=1.0">
        <style>
    header, footer {display:block;}
  </style>
  </head>
  <body>
    <header>
      Main Navigation here
    </header>
```

```
      body content here
      <footer>
        Footer links here
      </footer>
    </body>
  </html>
```

2. Now create another page with Modernizr included, and name it `ch01e4.html`:

```
<!doctype html>
<html>
  <head>
  <meta charset="utf-8">
  <meta name="viewport" content="width=device-width,
initial-scale=1.0">
    <script src="modernizr-1.7.min.js"></script>
    <style>
    header, footer {display:block;}
    </style>
  </head>
  <body>
    <header>
      Main Navigation here
    </header>
    body content here
    <footer>
      Footer links here
    </footer>
  </body>
</html>
```

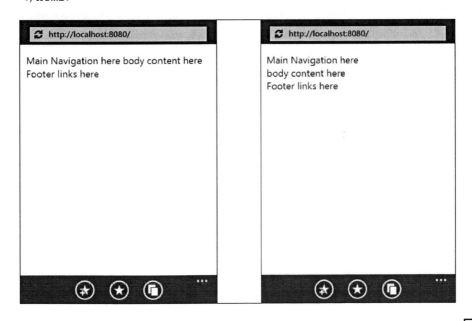

How it works...

Remember that if you use Modernizr for your project, you should always include it at the head of the file before the end of the `<head>` tag. There are other polyfills used for similar purposes, and some are listed in the following section.

There's more...

Modernizr is not the only script library helper out there; there are two other notable ones:

- **html5shim** by *Remy Sharp, Jonathan Neal & community*, enabled for print use, as well as at:

  `http://code.google.com/p/html5shim/`

- **innerShiv** by *Joe Bartlett*, enables elements for innerHTML use at:

  `http://jdbartlett.github.com/innershiv/`

HTML5 CSS reset

You may want to reset the set of new CSS HTML5 elements in your stylesheet:

```
article, aside, canvas, details, figcaption, figure,footer, header,
hgroup, menu, nav, section, summary,time, mark, audio, video {
   margin: 0;
   padding: 0;
   border: 0;
   font-size: 100%;
   font: inherit;
   vertical-align: baseline;
}
```

Enable block-level HTML5 elements in older IE

In your CSS, you might want to include the set of block-level HTML5 elements in your CSS reset. Do note that not all HTML5 elements have to be displayed as block elements.

Here is a list of block-level HTML5 elements:

```
article, aside, details, figcaption, figure,footer, header, hgroup,
menu, nav, section {
   display: block;
}
```

Modernizr

Modernizr does more than just making HTML5 elements stylable in CSS. It also helps to detect HTML5 feature support in the browser used for rendering. With version 2.0, you will have the option to customize the download `http://www.modernizr.com/download/`.

Designing for mobile

Target browser: all

For desktop design, one tends to use either fixed or fluid layout. On the mobile devices, one should almost always use fluid layout. Fluid layout could make your site responsive to browser resize.

Getting ready

Now create two empty HTML files in your text editor, name one of them `ch01r06_a.html` and the other `ch01r06_b.html`.

How to do it...

1. In `ch01r06_a.html`, enter the following code and save the file:

    ```
    <!doctype html>
    <html>
      <head>
      <meta name="viewport" content="width=device-width,
    initial-scale=1.0, maximum-scale=1.0">
        <script src="modernizr-1.7.min.js"></script>
        <style>
        body, #main ul, #main li, h1 {
          margin:0; padding:0;
        }
        body {
          background:#FFFFA6;
        }
        #container {
          font-family:Arial;
          width:300px;
          margin:0 auto;
        }
        header, footer {
          display:block;
        }
        #main li{
          list-style:none;
          height:40px;
          background:#29D9C2;
          margin-bottom:0.5em;
          line-height:40px;
    ```

```
      -moz-border-radius: 15px;
      -webkit-border-radius: 15px;
      border-radius: 15px;
    }
    #main li a {
      color:white;
      text-decoration:none;
      margin-left:1em;
    }
    </style>
    </head>
    <body>
      <div id="container">
        <header>
          <h1>Title here</h1>
        </header>
        <nav id="main">
          <ul>
            <li><a href="#">Home</a></li>
            <li><a href="#">Contact Us</a></li>
            <li><a href="#">Location</a></li>
            <li><a href="#">Product</a></li>
            <li><a href="#">About</a></li>
          </ul>
        </nav>
        <footer>
          Footer links here
        </footer>
      </div>
    </body>
</html>
```

2. In ch01r06_b.html, enter the following code and save the document:

```
<!doctype html>
<html>
  <head>
  <meta name="viewport" content="width=device-width,
initial-scale=1.0, maximum-scale=1.0">
  <script src="modernizr-1.7.min.js"></script>
  <style>
  body, #main ul, #main li, h1 {
    margin:0;
    padding:0;
  }
```

```
body {
  background:#FFFFA6;
}
#container {
  font-family:Arial;
  margin:0 10px;
}
header, footer {
  display:block;
}
#main li{
  list-style:none;
  height:40px;
  background:#29D9C2;
  margin-bottom:0.5em;
  line-height:40px;
  -moz-border-radius: 15px;
  -webkit-border-radius: 15px;
  border-radius: 15px;
}
#main li a {
  color:white;
  text-decoration:none;
  margin-left:1em;
}
</style>
</head>
<body>
  <div id="container">
    <header>
      <h1>Title here</h1>
    </header>
    <nav id="main">
      <ul>
        <li><a href="#">Home</a></li>
        <li><a href="#">Contact Us</a></li>
        <li><a href="#">Location</a></li>
        <li><a href="#">Product</a></li>
        <li><a href="#">About</a></li>
      </ul>
    </nav>
    <footer>
      Footer links here
    </footer>
  </div>
</body>
</html>
```

How it works...

When you view the two sites in portrait mode, they both look pretty much the same:

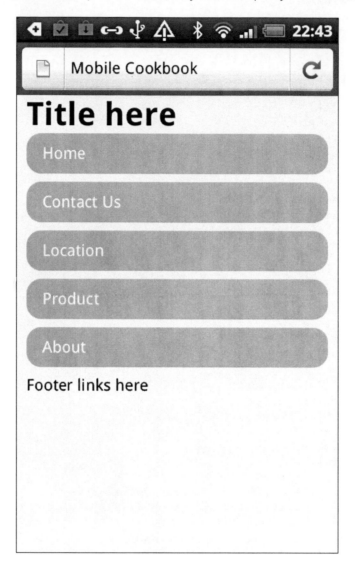

Now try rotating your screen and see what happens.

As you can see now, in landscape mode, the first example renders with spaces at the left and right side, and the second example covers most of the space of the screen:

The second example shows a different result:

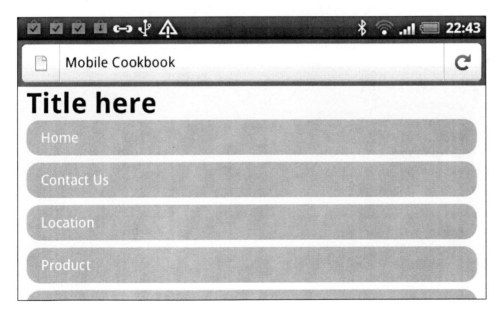

This site page looks very awkward in a fixed layout, but looks normal in a fluid layout. So when you design for mobile, always remember that your site should be designed with this flexibility. The reasons are:

- Mobile has both portrait and landscape mode
- Mobile has very limited space, so you should use every pixel available on the screen

There's more...

CSS media queries is also an essential part of responsive design. It assists you with the flexibility of mobile design.

```html
<!doctype html>
<html>
  <head>
  <meta name="viewport" content="width=device-width,
initial-scale=1.0, maximum-scale=1.0">
  <script src="modernizr-1.7.min.js"></script>
  <style>
  body {
    margin:0;
    padding:0;
    background:#FFFFA6;
  }

  #main section {
    display:block;
    border:5px solid #29D9C2;
    width:60%;
    height:120px;
    margin:5% auto;
  }

  @media screen and (min-width: 480px) {
    #main {
      width:90%;
      margin:0 auto;
    }

    #main > section:first-child {
      margin-right:5%;
    }

    #main section {
      float:left;
```

```
      width:45%;
    }
  }
  </style>
  </head>
  <body>
    <div id="container">

      <div id="main">
        <section id="top-news"></section>
        <section id="sports"></section>
      </div>

    </div>
  </body>
</html>
```

When rendered in a narrower screen, the two sections will be laid out vertically, when rendered in a wider screen, the two sections will be laid out horizontally. The technique we used to make this happen is by using CSS media queries. As in this example, we used @ media screen and (min-width: 480px) {..}, so what it means is that the page is rendered on a page that has a minimum width of 480px, the styles within will be applied:

Now let's see it in orientation mode, as shown next. The two boxes are now next to each other.

Desktop-first site

Apart from the idea of building a purely mobile or desktop site, there have also always been other ways. One of those is to build a desktop site first, and make it degrade gracefully in mobile.

Mobile-first site

Another approach is to build it 'mobile first' but make it render gracefully on the desktop.

One such approach uses the following in the CSS:

```
@media only screen and (min-width: 320px) {
  /* Styles */
}
@media only screen and (min-width: 640px) {
  /* Styles */
}
@media only screen and (min-width: 800px) {
  /* Styles */
}
@media only screen and (min-width: 1024px) {
  /* Styles */
}
```

One web approach

A third approach is to have a 'one web' version, by which, instead of focusing on mobile or desktop, you focus on both.

Defining a content strategy

Target browser: all

With the data you gathered from the analytics tools, you can define a strategy towards what you want to build. This is particularly useful if you already have a desktop version of the website.

Getting ready

Make sure you already have JavaScript embedded on your site.

How to do it...

1. Go to your analytics tool and click on **Visitors | Mobile** under the left navigation:

2. Now if you click on **Mobile Devices**, you can see the most common devices that people use to surf your site:

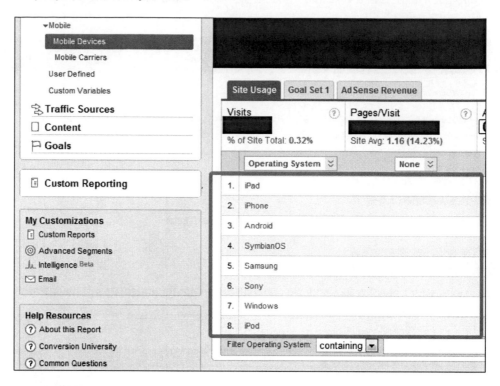

How it works...

Google Analytics can help in finding out the most commonly used mobile devices accessing your site, and also find out the most popular sections of your website.

There's more...

You can also determine what are the most useful pages on your mobile site. People treat mobile surfing differently from desktop surfing. For instance, if you are running a local store selling products, most people on a tend to surf pages like **Contact Us**, **Location**, and **Services** mobile device. Conversely, on a desktop, people tend to search for **Product Catalog**, **About**, and **Product Description**. Google Analytics can help you find out which are the most visited sections/pages on your site. Apart from Google Analytics, you can also use PercentMobile, as we saw earlier.

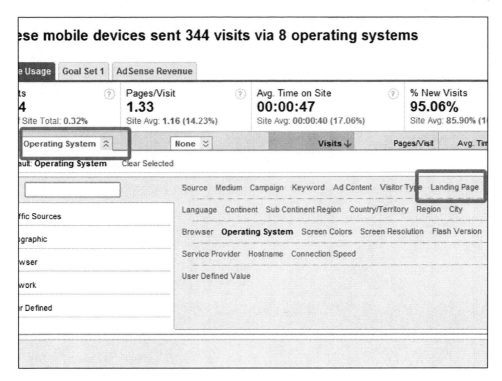

Browser grade

Using an analytics service is one way to decide which devices you want to support. Another way is to use browser grade to know what category you should be targeting. jQuery Mobile has an awesome grid support chart at `http://jquerymobile.com/gbs/`. There is also a slide on jQuery Mobile that talks about the overall strategies regarding mobile browser web development at `http://www.slideshare.net/jeresig/testing-mobile-javascript`.

Mobile matrices

I have been collaborating with *Jonathan Neal*, and many others, on Smartphone frontend matrices. You can have a look at:

`https://github.com/h5bp/mobile-boilerplate/wiki/Mobile-Matrices`

It contains information about most Smartphones in the market, their screen dimensions, DPI, and operating systems.

2
Mobile Setup and Optimization

In this chapter, we will cover:

- ▸ Adding a home screen button icon
- ▸ Preventing text resize
- ▸ Optimizing viewport width
- ▸ Fixing Mobile Safari screen scale
- ▸ Launching phone-specific programs from the browser
- ▸ Enabling iPhone start screen in full screen mode
- ▸ Preventing iOS from zooming onfocus
- ▸ Disabling or limiting WebKit features

Introduction

While there are many operating systems (OS) as well as device makers, inevitably there could be cross-browser issues that cost us a lot of headaches. But on the other hand, we developers love the challenges and set out to tackle them!

Throughout this chapter, we will first focus on cross-browser/browser-specific setup and optimizations you may want to consider. We will then go on to look at a couple of general/browser-specific features you may want to add at the start of your mobile development.

Adding a home screen button icon

Target devices: iOS, Android, Symbian

On modern smartphones, screens are mostly touch based. The iPhone revolutionized the way we think of mobile by making everything on your device an "app"; even SMS and phone dialing behave like apps with an icon on the home screen. For an HTML web app, things are a bit different; users have to go to a browser app first, type in the address and then launch your site. This can be too much hassle from a user perspective, so on certain smartphones, users can bookmark a home screen icon to a particular web app, so they can launch that particular web app site directly from the icon on their home screen.

That sounds cool, right? Yes, it does, but there are also issues associated with it. Not all browsers behave the same way when it comes to touch icons. In this recipe, we will examine the behavior of each browser and how to make home screen icons available to as many mobile browsers as possible.

Getting ready

First, you have to download the icon sets from the chapter code folder. If you open up the folder, you should be able to see the following:

```
apple-touch-icon.png
apple-touch-icon-57x57-precomposed.png
apple-touch-icon-72x72-precomposed.png
apple-touch-icon-114x114-precomposed.png
apple-touch-icon-precomposed.png
```

These images will be used for different devices.

Create an HTML document and name it `ch02r01.html`.

How to do it...

In your HTML document, use the following code:

```
<!doctype html>
<html>
  <head>
    <title>Mobile Cookbook</title>
```

```
    <meta charset="utf-8">
    <meta name="viewport" content="width=device-width, initial-
scale=1.0">
    <link rel="apple-touch-icon-precomposed" sizes="114x114"
href="icons/apple-touch-icon-114x114-precomposed.png">
    <link rel="apple-touch-icon-precomposed" sizes="72x72"
href="icons/apple-touch-icon-72x72-precomposed.png">
    <link rel="apple-touch-icon-precomposed" href="icons/apple-touch-
icon-precomposed.png">
    <link rel="shortcut icon" href="icons/apple-touch-icon.png">
  </head>
  <body>


  </body>
</html>
```

How it works...

Now let's break down the code:

As of iOS 4.2.1, it's possible to specify multiple icons for different device resolutions by using the `sizes` attribute.

```
<link rel="apple-touch-icon-precomposed" sizes="114x114" href="apple-
touch-icon-114x114-precomposed.png">
```

For high resolution retina displays on iPhone 4, a 114 x 114 icon is used.

```
<link rel="apple-touch-icon-precomposed" sizes="72x72" href="apple-
touch-icon-72x72-precomposed.png">
```

For iPad, a 72 x 72 icon can be used. For non-retina iPhone, Android 2.1+ devices, a 57 x 57 low resolution icon is used.

```
<link rel="apple-touch-icon-precomposed" href="apple-touch-icon-
precomposed.png">
```

For Nokia Symbian 60 devices, a `shortcut icon` is used in link relation to tell the device about the shortcut icon.

```
<link rel="shortcut icon" href="img/l/apple-touch-icon.png">
```

Here is what the bookmark looks like on Android:

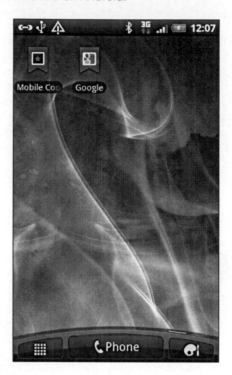

There's more...

There must be a couple of questions in your mind after seeing the previous example:

> ▸ Isn't it possible to define more than one value in the `rel` attribute? So can we combine the last two lines into something as follows?
>
> ```
> <link rel="shortcut icon apple-touch-icon-precomposed"
> href="apple-touch-icon-precomposed.png">
> ```
>
> It was tested, but somehow mobile browsers couldn't recognize the value.
>
> You might have seen people use:
>
> ```
> <link rel="apple-touch-icon-precomposed" media="screen and
> (min-resolution: 150dpi)" href="apple-touch-icon-114x114-
> precomposed.png">
> ```

Together with *Paul Irish* and *Divya Manian*, we have been working on Mobile Boilerplate (`http://www.h5bp.com/mobile`) that provides a rock-solid default for frontend mobile development. In Mobile Boilerplate, we have covered all the current scenarios and possible future scenarios:

```
https://github.com/h5bp/mobile-boilerplate/blob/master/index.html#L21
```

Everything you always wanted to know about touch icons

Most ideas presented on this topic are originated from *Mathias Bynens*. His original article *Everything you always wanted to know about touch icons* can be found at: `http://mathiasbynens.be/notes/touch-icons`.

Official documentation about Apple touch icons

There is a list of official documentation where you can find more information about touch icons for each specific device and browser:

- Apple touch icon:

  ```
  http://developer.apple.com/library/safari/#documentation/
  AppleApplications/Reference/SafariWebContent/
  ConfiguringWebApplications/ConfiguringWebApplications.html
  ```

- Official information from WHATWG:

  ```
  http://www.whatwg.org/specs/web-apps/current-work/multipage/
  links.html#rel-icon
  ```

Apple Custom Icon and Image Creation Guidelines

Guidelines and articles about how to create a touch icon can be found at the following article:

- Apple – *Custom Icon and Image Creation Guidelines:*

  ```
  http://developer.apple.com/library/ios/#documentation/
  userexperience/conceptual/mobilehig/IconsImages/IconsImages.
  html#//apple_ref/doc/uid/TP40006556-CH14-SW11
  ```

See also

Enabling iPhone start screen in full screen mode – in this recipe, we will see how to add a start screen in full screen mode when launched from the home screen touch icon.

Preventing text resize

Target devices: iOS, Windows Mobile

On certain mobile devices like the iPhone and Windows Mobile, browser text may resize when you rotate the device from portrait to landscape mode. This could be problematic to web developers because we want to have full control of the design and rendering of the website.

Getting ready

Create a new HTML file, and name it `ch02r02.html`. Enter the following code:

```html
<!doctype html>
<html>
  <head>
  <meta charset="utf-8">
  <meta name="viewport" content="width=device-width,
initial-scale=1.0, maximum-scale=1.0, minimum-scale=1.0">
  <style>
    figure, figcaption, header {
      display:block;
      margin:0 auto;
      text-align:center;
    }
  </style>
  </head>
  <body>
    <header>
      HTML5 Logo
    </header>
    <figure>
      <img src="HTML5_Badge_128.png" alt="HTML5 Badge" />
      <figcaption>
        It stands strong and true, resilient and universal as
the markup you write.
        It shines as bright and as bold as the forward-thinking,
dedicated web developers you are.
        It's the standard's standard, a pennant for progress.
        And it certainly doesn't use tables for layout.
      </figcaption>
    </figure>

  </body>
</html>
```

Now render this page in portrait mode in iPhone, as you can see, it will be rendered normally as follows:

Now if you render it in the landscape mode, the font size will suddenly increase. As we can see when the page is changed to landscape mode, the text will get resized. This is not the desired behavior. The following shows how it looks:

How to do it...

You can follow these steps to fix the issue:

1. You can add the following lines to the CSS, and then render the page in landscape again:

    ```
    html {
        -webkit-text-size-adjust: none;
    }
    ```

2. As You can see, the text now appears normal:

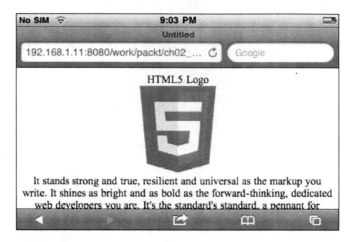

How it works...

To solve this issue, you have to add a CSS property named `text-size-adjust` in WebKit, and assign the value to `none` to prevent the auto adjust.

Setting `text-size-adjust` to none solves the problem for mobile-specific websites, but if we render this on a desktop screen or other non-mobile browser, the desktop browser text zoom feature will be disabled. To prevent this accessibility issue, we can set `text-size-adjust` to `100%` instead of `none`.

So we can tweak this example to:

```
html {
    -webkit-text-size-adjust: 100%;
}
```

There's more...

Apart from iPhone, other devices also have ways to add the text size adjust property.

Windows Mobile

Windows Mobile IE uses a different prefix. They originally added the WebKit prefix. The intent was adding support for the WebKit-specific property to make web developers' lives a bit easier by not having to add yet another vendor-prefixed CSS property to their pages to control how text was scaled. Even more specifically, they intuited that the most common use case for this property was to explicitly set it to none in order to tell the browser not to scale a particular section of the text.

After hearing the community's feedback on this issue (and a couple of face-plants when they realized the broader implications of implementing other browser vendors' CSS properties) they've decided that it's best to only implement the -ms- prefixed version and not the -webkit- one.

So to make the preceding example more complete, you can add:

```
html {
  -webkit-text-size-adjust: 100%;
  -ms-text-size-adjust: 100%;
}
```

Making it future proof

To make things more future proof, you can add one more line without any prefix, as follows:

```
html {
  -webkit-text-size-adjust: 100%;
  -ms-text-size-adjust: 100%;
  text-size-adjust: 100%;
}
```

px em, which is better?

The common debate about using px versus em is less of a problem on mobile. Originally Yahoo! User Interface used ems for the reason that IE6 doesn't support page zoom with pixels. On mobile, there isn't such an issue, and even if we want the page to render well on desktop browsers, the likelihood of someone using IE6 is getting lower and lower, so in most cases, you can save the trouble of using ems and all the calculation, and choose instead to use pixels.

Optimizing viewport width

Target device: cross-browser

Different mobile devices have different default mobile viewport widths. Refer to Appendix X for a complete list of default viewport widths for all mobile devices. If you leave it unset, in most cases, it will cause an unexpected result. For example, in an iPhone if the viewport width is left unset, it will be rendered as 980 px.

Getting ready

Let's create an HTML document and name it `ch02r03.html`.

How to do it...

Here is what we can do to optimize the viewport width:

1. Add the following code to `ch02r03.html` and render it in your mobile browser:

```
<!doctype html>
<html>
  <head>
  <meta charset="utf-8">

  </head>
  <body>
    <header>
      HTML5 Logo
    </header>
    <div id="main">
    <h1>Lorem ipsum</h1>
Lorem ipsum dolor sit amet, consectetur adipisicing elit, sed do
eiusmod tempor incididunt ut labore et dolore magna aliqua. Ut
enim ad minim veniam, quis nostrud exercitation ullamco laboris
nisi ut aliquip ex ea commodo consequat. Duis aute irure dolor
in reprehenderit in voluptate velit esse cillum dolore eu fugiat
nulla pariatur. Excepteur sint occaecat cupidatat non proident,
sunt in culpa qui officia deserunt mollit anim id est laborum.
    </div>

  </body>
</html>
```

Here is how it's rendered by default:

2. If we render this example, we can see that everything becomes extremely small. Now, let's set the viewport width to the device width:

```
<!doctype html>
<html>
  <head>
  <meta charset="utf-8">
  <meta name="viewport" content="width=device-width">

  </head>
  <body>
    <header>
      HTML5 Logo
    </header>
<div id="main">
```

```
    <h1>Lorem ipsum</h1>
<p>Lorem ipsum dolor sit amet, consectetur adipisicing elit, sed
do eiusmod tempor incididunt ut labore et dolore magna aliqua. Ut
enim ad minim veniam, quis nostrud exercitation ullamco laboris
nisi ut aliquip ex ea commodo consequat. Duis aute irure dolor
in reprehenderit in voluptate velit esse cillum dolore eu fugiat
nulla pariatur. Excepteur sint occaecat cupidatat non proident,
sunt in culpa qui officia deserunt mollit anim id est laborum.</p>
    </div>


    </body>
</html>
```

Now the content width uses the screen width and the text becomes readable:

How it works...

When we set viewport width to device-width, it will tell the browser not to scale the page to fix the device area. So for iPhone, the `device-width` is 320 px in portrait mode and 480 px in landscape mode.

There's more...

For some really old relic mobile browsers, the `meta` attribute isn't recognized. To deal with these browsers, you need to use:

```
<meta name="HandheldFriendly" content="true">
```

This is used by older versions of Palm OS, AvantGo, and Blackberry.

```
<meta name="MobileOptimized" content="320">
```

For Microsoft PocketPC, a `MobileOptimized` attribute was introduced.

So the most complete code should look like:

```
<meta name="HandheldFriendly" content="true">
<meta name="MobileOptimized" content="320">
<meta name="viewport" content="width=device-width">
```

IE for Windows Phone viewport blog post

On IE for Windows Phone Team Weblog, there is an article about *IE Mobile Viewport on Windows Phone 7*. In it, the author has explained important information like how Windows Phone 7 implements "device-width", together with much other very useful information in general. You can read the article here: `http://blogs.msdn.com/b/iemobile/archive/2010/11/22/the-ie-mobile-viewport-on-windows-phone-7.aspx`.

Safari documentation

Safari has a reference in the developer's library at: `http://developer.apple.com/library/safari/#documentation/appleapplications/reference/SafariHTMLRef/Articles/MetaTags.html`.

Blackberry documentation

There is a Blackberry Browser Content Design Guidelines document. It explains Blackberry's use of viewport width: `http://docs.blackberry.com/en/developers/deliverables/4305/BlackBerry_Browser-4.6.0-US.pdf`.

Fixing Mobile Safari screen re-flow scale

Target device: iOS

Mobile Safari has an annoying screen re-flow bug: When you rotate the mobile browser from portrait mode to landscape mode, the text will suddenly jump to a bigger size.

During the time I was working on building Mobile Boilerplate, *Jeremy Keith* and I had a long discussion on this issue.

The traditional way of fixing this is to add the following scaling attributes to the `meta` viewport:

```
<meta name="viewport" content="width=device-width, initial-scale=1.0,
maximum-scale=1.0, minimum-scale=1.0">
```

This solution was first incorporated into Mobile Boilerplate. *Jeremy* pointed out that this solves the scale jump problem, but at the same time, it causes another issue with accessibility: When you set the values as shown above, you can no longer zoom the page to enlarge it. For people with eyesight problems, the ability to zoom is essential. But if we let the zoom happen, the text jump will annoy the majority of the users. So, for a long time it was an accessibility versus usability debate.

I discovered a method that could tackle the issue and we will discuss this next.

Getting ready

First, let's create an HTML document and name it `ch02r04.html`, enter the following code in it:

```
<!doctype html>
<html>
  <head>
  <meta charset="utf-8">
  <meta name="viewport" content="width=device-width, initial-
scale=1.0">
  </head>
  <body>

  <div>
  <h1>Lorem ipsum</h1>
<p>Lorem ipsum dolor sit amet, consectetur adipisicing elit, sed
do eiusmod tempor incididunt ut labore et dolore magna aliqua. Ut
enim ad minim veniam, quis nostrud exercitation ullamco laboris
nisi ut aliquip ex ea commodo consequat. Duis aute irure dolor in
reprehenderit in voluptate velit esse cillum dolore eu fugiat nulla
pariatur. Excepteur sint occaecat cupidatat non proident, sunt in
culpa qui officia deserunt mollit anim id est laborum.</p>
  </div>
  </body>
</html>
```

This page renders perfectly fine in portrait mode:

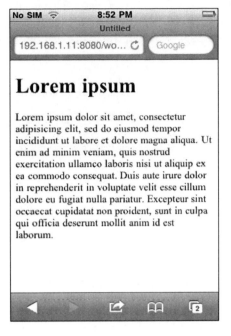

But when displayed in landscape mode, things change:

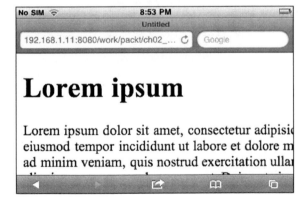

How to do it...

All we need to do to solve this problem is to dynamically reset the scale factors to default when the user zooms in on the page. Now put the following code in your HTML document:

```html
<!doctype html>
<html>
  <head>
  <meta charset="utf-8">
  <meta name="viewport" content="width=device-width, initial-scale=1.0">
  </head>
  <body>


  <div>
  <h1>Lorem ipsum</h1>
<p>Lorem ipsum dolor sit amet, consectetur adipisicing elit, sed
do eiusmod tempor incididunt ut labore et dolore magna aliqua. Ut
enim ad minim veniam, quis nostrud exercitation ullamco laboris
nisi ut aliquip ex ea commodo consequat. Duis aute irure dolor in
reprehenderit in voluptate velit esse cillum dolore eu fugiat nulla
pariatur. Excepteur sint occaecat cupidatat non proident, sunt in
culpa qui officia deserunt mollit anim id est laborum.</p>
  </div>
    <script>
      var metas = document.getElementsByTagName('meta');
      var i;
      if (navigator.userAgent.match(/iPhone/i)) {
        for (i=0; i<metas.length; i++) {
          if (metas[i].name == "viewport") {
            metas[i].content = "width=device-width, minimum-scale=1.0,
maximum-scale=1.0";
          }
        }
        document.addEventListener("gesturestart", gestureStart,
false);
      }
      function gestureStart() {
        for (i=0; i<metas.length; i++) {
          if (metas[i].name == "viewport") {
            metas[i].content = "width=device-width, minimum-
scale=0.25, maximum-scale=1.6";
          }
        }
      }
    </script>
  </body>
</html>
```

Now if we rotate the screen from portrait to landscape, the issue should no longer exist, and if we zoom in on the page, it will react as expected:

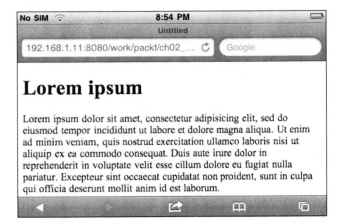

How it works...

Let's have a walk through of the code to see how it works.

1. We need to know the default minimum-scale and maximum-scale values. In the iPhone's official documentation, it states that the minimum-scale value is 0.25, and the maximum-scale value is 1.6. So to replace the default value, we need to set:

```
function gestureStart() {
  var metas = document.getElementsByTagName('meta');
  var i;
  for (i=0; i if (metas[i].name == "viewport") {
    metas[i].content = "width=device-width, minimum-scale=0.25, maximum-scale=1.6";
  }
}
```

2. Next, we need to know when to set this. This is very easy: The iPhone has a gesture event listener we can use to target the document body. Here is how to do so:

```
document.addEventListener("gesturestart", gestureStart, false);
```

3. Finally, we need to make sure this only happens on iPhone. Again this can be easily done using:

```
if (navigator.userAgent.match(/iPhone/i)) {
document.addEventListener("gesturestart", gestureStart, false);
}
```

There's more...

If you are interested to know the whole story and discussion between Jeremy and I, you can read it at `http://www.blog.highub.com/mobile-2/a-fix-for-iphone-viewport-scale-bug/`.

Even though this provides a fix for the issue, there are a couple of problems that some people experience:

- ▶ As soon as the user makes a gesture on the document, zooming is enabled again. So if you change the device orientation after that, the zoom bug will still occur.
- ▶ It's reported on iOS4 that users can only effectively start zooming after starting a second gesture.

A slightly improved version

Mathias Bynens has a revised version with smarter coding. You can see the code at

`https://gist.github.com/901295`.

An even better version

John-David Dalton had an even better updated version with smarter and leaner code at

`https://gist.github.com/903131`.

A word for jQuery Mobile

Scott Jehl from jQuery Mobile mentioned it might be implemented in jQuery Mobile in the future. Currently, you could see his gist at `https://gist.github.com/1183357`.

Launching phone-specific programs from the browser

Target device: cross-browser

One can launch phone-specific programs from the mobile browser such as Maps, Call, and SMS can be launched from certain mobile devices. Whether the program can be launched depends on the availability of the native application on the particular device.

Getting ready

Create an HTML document and name it `ch02r05.html`.

How to do it...

Here is how we could launch a phone-specific program:

1. Let's add the following code to the HTML document:

```
<!doctype html>
<html>
  <head>
  <meta charset="utf-8">
  <meta name="viewport" content="width=device-width,
initial-scale=1.0">
  </head>
  <body>
    <header>
       HTML5 Logo
    </header>
  <div>
    <h1>Lorem ipsum</h1>
    <a href="http://maps.google.com/maps?q=cupertino">
Directions</a>
  </div>

  </body>
</html>
```

2. Now run this code in Palm OS browser, press the address link. You will be prompted to launch the map application on your phone:

How it works...

Unlike some schemes, map URLs do not start with a "maps" scheme identifier. Instead, map links are specified as regular HTTP links, but are targeted at the Google Maps servers. The device browser will be able to tell if it's a map and launch the program with the information parsed.

There's more...

You can do more than just launch an application. The following examples show the strings you would use to provide driving directions between San Francisco and Cupertino:

```
<a href="http://maps.google.com/maps?daddr=San+Francisco,+CA&saddr=cu
pertino">Directions</a>
```

So, what if a browser can't launch a specific program? That's ok! In this case it will just open as a normal link:

Mobile Safari URL scheme

A list of all Mobile Safari-related URL schemes can be found at: `http://developer.apple.com/library/safari/#featuredarticles/iPhoneURLScheme_Reference/Introduction/Introduction.html`.

Blackberry URL scheme

A list of all Blackberry-related URL schemes can be found at: `http://docs.blackberry.com/en/developers/deliverables/18169/`.

Sony Ericsson developers' guidelines

Sony Ericsson developers can download *Web Browsing Developer Guidelines* from the Developer World site at: `http://developer.sonyericsson.com/wportal/devworld/search-downloads?cat=%5B1.706817%2C+1.716594%2C+1.716688%5D&cc=gb&lc=en`.

Enabling iPhone start screen in full screen mode

Target-device: iOS

To make a web app feel more like a native app, the iPhone has quite a few unique features for developers to add on web apps. You can add start screen in full screen mode, and style the status bar, as well as defining a pre-load screen for the app.

Getting ready

Download the images in the source code provided, create an HTML document, and name it `ch02r06.html`.

How to do it...

Here is how we can make the start screen in full screen mode:

1. Enter the following HTML code:

```
<!doctype html>
<html>
  <head>
  <meta charset="utf-8">
  <meta name="viewport" content="width=device-width, initial-
scale=1.0">
  <meta name="apple-mobile-web-app-capable" content="yes">
  <meta name="apple-mobile-web-app-status-bar-style"
content="black">
  <link rel="apple-touch-startup-image" href="img/l/splash.png">
  </head>
  <body>
    <header>
      HTML5 Logo
    </header>
    <div>
      Lorem ipsum
    </div>

  </body>
</html>
```

2. If you bookmark the page and open it in the browser from the app icon, it will display as a full-screen app.

How it works...

Let's go through the code:

```
<meta name="apple-mobile-web-app-capable" content="yes">
```

This makes the web page run in full screen mode when launched from the home screen icon, hides the address bar and component bar at the browser's top and bottom.

```
<meta name="apple-mobile-web-app-status-bar-style" content="black">
```

This styles the status bar at the top of browser.

```
<link rel="apple-touch-startup-image" href="img/l/splash.png">
```

You can also add a splash screen when the app launches, which is a preload screen displayed while the page is still loading.

There's more...

iPad and iPhone have different splash screen sizes, so if we want the site to dynamically change the splash screen, this depends on the browser used to render. We can use the following JavaScript function to do this:

```
var filename = navigator.platform === 'iPad' ? 'h/' : 'l/';
    document.write('<link rel="apple-touch-startup-image" href="/img/'
+ filename + 'splash.png" />' );
```

Full screen issue with iOS 4.3

iOS 4.3 introduced a new feature which they call the JavaScript Nitro Engine. This new code allows the default Safari browser to load pages up to twice as fast. However, this feature didn't seem to be supported by full screen web applications. While some question why Apple didn't incorporate the new Safari feature with its web applications, others also point to evidence that it might just be a bug.

Safari documentation about web applications

For the official documentation, you can visit the site on Safari at:

```
http://developer.apple.com/library/safari/#documentation/
appleapplications/Reference/SafariWebContent/
ConfiguringWebApplications/ConfiguringWebApplications.html
```

Safari splash image and touch icon guidelines

For splash image and touch icon guidelines, you can visit Custom Icon and Image Creation Guidelines on the official Safari site:

```
http://developer.apple.com/library/safari/#documentation/
UserExperience/Conceptual/MobileHIG/IconsImages/IconsImages.html#//
apple_ref/doc/uid/TP40006556-CH14
```

Prevent iOS from zooming onfocus

Target device: iOS

In JavaScript events API, there is a `form onfocus` event. When you tap on a form element in iOS, the element will zoom in on the device screen. For a site not designed to be responsive or mobile-specific, such default zooming can be helpful, but for a site that is mobile optimized, this could be less helpful and can be annoying. To disable this default behavior, we could change the meta viewport value `onfocus` and `onblur`.

Getting ready

Create an HTML document and name it `ch02r06_b.html`.

How to do it...

Here is how we could launch a phone-specific program:

1. Let's add the following code to the HTML document:

```html
<!doctype html>
<html>
  <head>
  <meta charset="utf-8">
  <meta name="viewport" content="width=device-width, initial-scale=1.0">
  </head>
  <body>
  <form>

<label>First name:</label> <input type="text" name="fname" /><br />
<label>Last name:</label> <input type="text" name="lname" />
  </form>
  <script>
        var $viewportMeta = $('meta[name="viewport"]');
        $('input, select, textarea').bind('focus blur',
function(event) {
```

```
        $viewportMeta.attr('content', 'width=device-width,initial-
    scale=1,maximum-scale=' + (event.type == 'blur' ? 10 : 1));
            });
    </script>
    </body>
</html>
```

2. Now, render the page in the iOS devices, touch focus the form input field, and as you can see, now the input field won't zoom in.

How it works...

Now let's extract out the JavaScript portion:

```
<script>
        var $viewportMeta = $('meta[name="viewport"]');
        $('input, select, textarea').bind('focus blur',
function(event) {
    $viewportMeta.attr('content', 'width=device-width,initial-
scale=1,maximum-scale=' + (event.type == 'blur' ? 10 : 1));
        });
    </script>
```

What the script does is when the `onfocus` event is detected, we set the maximum-scale to 1 and when `onblur` is detected, we set it to 10.

There's more...

You can read more about the original blog post discussion at:

`http://nerd.vasilis.nl/prevent-ios-from-zooming-onfocus/`

This code snippet was added to Mobile Boilerplate:

`https://github.com/h5bp/mobile-boilerplate/blob/master/js/mylibs/`
`helper.js`

Disabling or limiting WebKit features

Target-device: WebKit mobile browsers (Android, iOS)

There are many device-specific issues in mobile browsers. With a few less-known CSS techniques, we could tackle these issues easily. Let's take a look at some of the issues and how we can magically get them fixed.

Getting ready

Create an HTML document and name it `ch02r07.html`.

How to do it...

Here is an example of how to limit the WebKit feature:

1. Add the following code into the HTML document:

```
<!doctype html>
<html>
  <head>
  <meta charset="utf-8">
  <meta name="viewport" content="width=device-width, initial-
scale=1.0">
  <meta name="apple-mobile-web-app-capable" content="yes">
  <style>
  .nocallout {-webkit-touch-callout: none;}
  #targetarea {width:200px; height:120px; padding-top:80px;
background:#ccc; text-align:center; font-size:20px;}
  </style>
  </head>
  <body>

    <div id="targetarea" class="nocallout">
      <a href="http://www.google.com" target="_blank">Google</a>
    </div>

  </body>
</html>
```

2. Now, enter the additional code to the HTML document,

```
<!doctype html>
<html>
 <head>
  <meta charset="utf-8">
  <meta name="viewport" content="width=device-width,
initial-scale=1.0">
 <meta name="apple-mobile-web-app-capable" content="yes">
 <style>
  .nocallout {-webkit-touch-callout: none;}
  #targetarea {width:200px; height:120px; padding-top:80px;
background:#ccc; text-align:center; font-size:20px;}
  </style>
  </head>
  <body>

    <div id="targetarea" class="nocallout">
      <a href="http://www.google.com" target="_blank">Google</a>
    </div>

  </body>
</html>
```

How it works...

Without setting `webkit-touch-callout`, when you tap and hold a link on your device, there will be a prompt asking you if you want to open it in the current page, open it in the new page or copy, as shown in the first example.

If you want to disable this feature, you can do so by setting `webkit-touch-callout` value to `none`, as shown in the second example.

There's more...

Another feature you might want to limit is the copy-and-paste. This feature makes sense on a web page, but for most interface elements of an application it is not wanted.

```
<style type="text/css">
  .oncopy {
    -webkit-user-select: text;
  }
</style>
```

Changing the tap color

You can change the tap color by using the following rule:

```
<style type="text/css">
  * {
    -webkit-tap-highlight-color: rgba(0,0,0,0);
  }
</style>
```

Making text area content editable

If you want to have an element as `contenteditable`, you can use the following CSS:

```
textarea.contenteditable {
  -webkit-appearance: none;
}
```

Ellipsis for the narrow screen

On mobile browsers, the screen is much narrower, so when you are displaying a menu title list, text overflow may occur. If this happens, a CSS trick could help you fix text overflow with ellipsis:

```
.ellipsis {
  text-overflow: ellipsis;
  overflow: hidden;
  white-space: nowrap;
}
```

3
Interactive Media with Mobile Events

In this chapter, we will cover:

- ▸ Moving an element with touch events
- ▸ Detecting and handling orientation event
- ▸ Rotating an HTML element with gesture events
- ▸ Making a carousel with swipe events
- ▸ Manipulating image zoom with gesture events

Introduction

One of the biggest differences between mobile and desktop is the way in which we interact with the screen. On a desktop screen, we use a mouse to move and click events to control the interaction. On a mobile screen, the interaction comes from touch and gesture events. In this chapter, we will see some of the events that are unique to touch screens (for example, two finger events) and how you can leverage these features to build something unique for mobile.

Moving an element with touch events

Target device: cross-browser

On a mobile screen, we interact with elements using touch events. Because of that, we can move an HTML element on the screen with our fingers.

Getting ready

For this example, we will be using jQuery. First, let's create a new HTML file, and name it `ch03r01.html`.

How to do it...

In your HTML document, use the following code:

```html
<!doctype html>
<html>
  <head>
    <title>Mobile Cookbook</title>
    <meta charset="utf-8">
    <meta name="viewport" content="width=device-width,
initial-scale=1.0">
    <style>
    #square {
      width: 100px;
      height: 100px;
      background:#ccc;
      position:absolute;
    }
    </style>
  </head>
  <body>

    <div id="main">
      <div id="square">
      </div>
    </div>

    <script src="http://code.jquery.com/jquery-1.5.2.min.js"></script>
    <script src="http://code.jquery.com/mobile/1.0a4.1/jquery.
mobile-1.0a4.1.min.js"></script>
    <script>
    $('#square').bind('touchmove',function(e){
      e.preventDefault();
      var touch = e.originalEvent.touches[0] || e.originalEvent.
changedTouches[0];
      var elm = $(this).offset();
      var x = touch.pageX - elm.left/2;
      var y = touch.pageY - elm.top/2;
     $(this).css('left', x+'px');
     $(this).css('top', y+'px');
     });
  </script>
  </body>
</html>
```

Now let's see how it renders in Opera:

How it works...

First, we register the square `div` with a `touchmove` event.

You can detect the touch position relative to the page which is `touch.pageX` and `touch.pageY` in our example. We use the finger position minus half the width and height of the square `div` element, so it feels like we are moving with the `div` center as the registration point.

```
var x = touch.pageX - elm.left/2;
var y = touch.pageY - elm.top/2;
```

We apply the x and y values to the square element using CSS position. This is the 'moving' action.

```
$(this).css('left', x+'px');
$(this).css('top', y+'px');
```

There's more...

You may have realized that, at the top of this example, there is one line as follows:

```
var touch = e.originalEvent.touches[0] || e.originalEvent.
changedTouches[0];
```

Now you might be wondering what it does. Mobile Safari does not allow the `e.touches` and `e.changedTouches` properties on event objects to be copied to another object. You can get around this issue by using `e.originalEvent`. You could read more about it here:

`http://www.the-xavi.com/articles/trouble-with-touch-events-jquery.`

jQuery mobile events

jQuery mobile is a set of components. If you want to dig into all the mobile-related events, you can find them at:

```
https://github.com/shichuan/jquery-mobile/blob/master/js/jquery.
mobile.event.js.
```

Zepto

Zepto is a more lightweight alternative to jQuery that you could consider using if your main target is WebKit-based browsers. You can find out more about it at:

```
https://github.com/madrobby/zepto.
```

Safari's guide on mobile event handling

For the official reference, you could visit Safari's online guide at:

```
http://developer.apple.com/library/safari/#documentation/
appleapplications/reference/safariwebcontent/HandlingEvents/
HandlingEvents.html.
```

See also

- ▶ *Redrawing a canvas with orientation events*
- ▶ *Rotating an HTML element with gesture events*
- ▶ *Making a carousel with swipe events*
- ▶ *Manipulating image zoom with gesture events*

Detecting and handling orientation event

Target device: cross-browser

On mobile browsers, if your site is built based on a fluid layout, it shouldn't be affected by orientation change. But for a highly interactive site, sometimes you may want to handle orientation change in a special way.

Getting ready

Create a new HTML file, and name it ch03r02.html.

How to do it...

Now let's start creating the HTML and Script to detect and handle orientation event.

1. Enter the following code:

```
<!doctype html>
<html>
  <head>
    <title>Mobile Cookbook</title>
    <meta charset="utf-8">
    <meta name="viewport" content="width=device-width,
initial-scale=1.0">
    <style>
    html, body {
      padding: none;
      margin: none;
    }
    </style>
    <link rel="stylesheet" href="http://code.jquery.com/
mobile/1.0/jquery.mobile-1.0.min.css" />
    <script src="http://code.jquery.com/jquery-1.6.4.min.js"></
script>
    <script src="http://code.jquery.com/mobile/1.0/jquery.mobile-
1.0.min.js"></script>
  </head>
  <body>
    <div id="a">
    </div>
    <script>
      var metas = document.getElementsByTagName('meta');
      var i;
      if (navigator.userAgent.match(/iPhone/i)) {
        for (i=0; i<metas.length; i++) {
          if (metas[i].name == "viewport") {
            metas[i].content = "width=device-width,
minimum-scale=1.0, maximum-scale=1.0";
          }
        }
        document.addEventListener("gesturestart", gestureStart,
false);
      }
      function gestureStart() {
        for (i=0; i<metas.length; i++) {
```

```
            if (metas[i].name == "viewport") {
                metas[i].content = "width=device-width,
minimum-scale=0.25, maximum-scale=1.6";
            }
          }
        }
      </script>

      <script>
        $(window).bind('orientationchange',function(event){
          updateOrientation(event.orientation);
        })
        function updateOrientation(orientation) {
          $("#a").html("<p>"+orientation.toUpperCase()+"</p>");
        }
      </script>
    </body>
</html>
```

2. Now, render this code in your mobile browser and rotate the screen to view in both portrait and landscape mode. In portrait mode, the text output will be 'PORTAIT'.

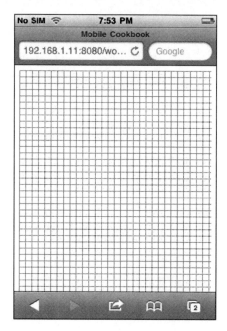

3. When we rotate the screen to landscape mode, the text will be 'LANDSCAPE'.

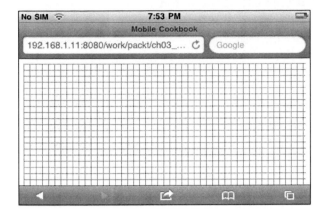

How it works...

By listening to `window.onorientationchange` event, we could get the `orientationchange` event, when it occurs; we get the `event.orientation` parsed to the function to output the result.

There's more...

At times, you may want to lock the orientation of the screen if let's say when building a game. For a native application, this can be easy, but for a web app, this can be a bit difficult to achieve.

Let's create a one-page screen that locks to only landscape mode. Note that this is a proof-of-concept, and to create really sophisticated apps or game requires more calculation and handling.

Create a document and name it `ch03r02_b.html`, and enter the following code

```
<!doctype html>
<html>
  <head>
    <title>Mobile Cookbook</title>
    <meta charset="utf-8">
    <meta name="viewport" content="width=device-width,
initial-scale=1.0">
    <link rel="stylesheet" href="css/style.css">

    <style>
    body {
      font-family: 'Kranky', serif;
      font-size: 36px;
```

```
      font-style: normal;
      font-weight: 400;


      word-spacing: 0em;
      line-height: 1.2;
    }
    html {
      background:#F1F2CE;
    }
    html, body, #screen {
      padding:0;
      margin:0;
    }
    #screen {
      text-align:center;
      -moz-transform:rotate(90deg);
      -webkit-transform:rotate(90deg);
      -o-transform:rotate(90deg);
      -ms-transform:rotate(90deg);
    }
    #screen div {
      padding-top:130px;
    }
    @media screen and (min-width: 321px){
      #screen {
        text-align:center;
        -moz-transform:rotate(0deg);
        -webkit-transform:rotate(0deg);
        -o-transform:rotate(0deg);
        -ms-transform:rotate(0deg);

      }
      #screen div {
        padding-top:70px;
      }
    }
    </style>
  </head>
  <body>
    <div id="screen">
      <div id="loader">enter the game</div>
    </div>
    <script>
      var metas = document.getElementsByTagName('meta');
      var i;
      if (navigator.userAgent.match(/iPhone/i)) {
```

```
        for (i=0; i<metas.length; i++) {
          if (metas[i].name == "viewport") {
            metas[i].content = "width=device-width, minimum-scale=1.0,
maximum-scale=1.0";
          }
        }
        document.addEventListener("gesturestart", gestureStart,
false);
      }
      function gestureStart() {
        for (i=0; i<metas.length; i++) {
          if (metas[i].name == "viewport") {
            metas[i].content = "width=device-width,
minimum-scale=0.25, maximum-scale=1.6";
          }
        }
      }
      window.onorientationchange = function() {
        update();
      }
      function update() {
        switch(window.orientation) {
          case 0:   // Portrait
          case 180: // Upside-down Portrait
            var cWidth = window.innerWidth;
            var cHeight = window.innerHeight;
            document.getElementById("screen").style.width = cHeight-
36+'px';
            document.getElementById("screen").style.height =
cWidth+'px';
            break;
          case -90: // Landscape: turned 90 degrees counter-clockwise
          case 90:  // Landscape: turned 90 degrees clockwise
            var cWidth = window.innerWidth;
            var cHeight = window.innerHeight;
            document.getElementById("screen").style.width = "100%";
            document.getElementById("screen").style.height = "auto";
            break;
        }
      }
      update();
    </script>

  </body>
</html>
```

Now if you render the page in your browser, you will see the following screen. In portrait mode, it suggests to the user the game/application is designed to be viewed in landscape mode:

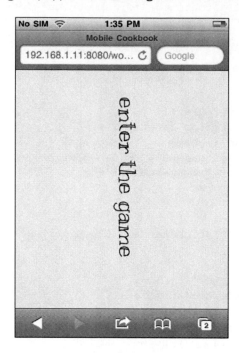

When you rotate the screen from portrait to landscape mode, it looks normal:

In this example, we used `transform:rotate` from CSS3 to rotate the screen to 90 degrees when viewed in portrait mode:

```
#screen {
  text-align:center;
  -moz-transform:rotate(90deg);
  -webkit-transform:rotate(90deg);
  -o-transform:rotate(90deg);
  -ms-transform:rotate(90deg);
}
```

The mode the user is in can be determined by `window.orientation`. There are four values: -90, 0, 90, 180. The device is in landscape mode when the degree is -90 and 90. And it's in portrait mode when the degree is 0 and 180.

```
switch(window.orientation) {
  case 0:   // Portrait
  case 180: // Upside-down Portrait
  //...
  break;
  case -90: // Landscape: turned 90 degrees counter-clockwise
  case 90:  // Landscape: turned 90 degrees clockwise
  //...
  break;
}
```

With this, you can determine the orientation of the screen.

Safari's native support

For the official reference, you could visit Safari's online guide at:

`http://developer.apple.com/library/safari/#documentation/appleapplications/reference/safariwebcontent/HandlingEvents/HandlingEvents.html`.

Web versus native

Although mobile web is catching up, if you are developing a highly interactive application, always keep in mind that even the slowest native app still performs faster than an HTML app. If you are deciding to use HTML5 to build an app, you also have to keep all the hacks and browser inconsistencies in mind.

See also

- ▸ *Moving an element with touch events*
- ▸ *Rotating an HTML element with gesture events*
- ▸ *Making a carousel with swipe events*
- ▸ *Zooming an image with gesture events*

Rotating an HTML element with gesture events

Target device: iOS, Android, Symbian

On Mobile Safari, you can detect the degrees of rotation when people use two fingers to do a rotation on the screen. Because of that, we can use our fingers to rotate an element on the screen!

Getting ready

Let's create an HTML document and name it ch03r03.html.

How to do it...

1. Add the following code to ch03r03.html and render it in your mobile browser:

```
<!doctype html>
<html>
  <head>
    <title>Mobile Cookbook</title>
    <meta charset="utf-8">
    <meta name="viewport" content="width=device-width,
initial-scale=1.0, maximum-scale=1.0">
    <style>
    #main {
      text-align:center;
    }
    #someElm {
      margin-top:50px;
      margin-left:50px;
```

```
      width: 200px;
      height: 200px;
      background:#ccc;
      position:absolute;
    }
   </style>
 </head>
 <body>

   <div id="main">
     <div id="someElm">
     </div>
   </div>


   <script>
   var rotation =0 ;
   var node = document.getElementById('someElm');

   node.ongesturechange = function(e){

     var node = e.target;
     //alert(e.rotation);
     // scale and rotation are relative values,
     // so we wait to change our variables until the gesture ends
     node.style.webkitTransform = "rotate(" + ((rotation +
e.rotation) % 360) + "deg)";
     //alert("rotate(" + ((rotation + e.rotation) % 360) +
"deg)");
   }

   node.ongestureend = function(e){
     // Update the values for the next time a gesture happens
     rotation = (rotation + e.rotation) % 360;
   }
   </script>
 </body>
</html>
```

2. Now use two fingers to rotate the box and you will see something like this:

How it works...

In this example, we rotate the element when there is an `ongesturechange` event triggered. We get the rotation degree by using the following value:

```
e.target.rotation
```

There's more...

You may have noticed that we also listen to `ongestureend` event, because if the user has previously rotated, this script will remember the last rotated angle and continue to rotate from there.

Safari event handling

For the official reference, you could visit Safari's online guide at:

```
http://developer.apple.com/library/safari/#documentation/
appleapplications/reference/safariwebcontent/HandlingEvents/
HandlingEvents.html.
```

CSS3 transforms

In this example, we used CSS3's transforms feature. You can find more information about WebKit and CSS transform at WebKit's blog at:

```
http://www.webkit.org/blog/130/css-transforms/.
```

Drawbacks of the scale bug fix

In this example, we used `maximum-scale=1.0` to prevent zooming when using a gesture event. This will cause some accessibility drawbacks, so use a rotate event only if you are building a highly interactive web application. Try to avoid it when building a mobile website.

See also

- *Moving an element with touch events*
- *Redrawing a canvas with orientation events*
- *Rotating an HTML element with gesture events*
- Zooming an image with gesture events

Making a carousel with swipe events

One of the common features of mobile devices is swiping. When you browse photos in your photo gallery, you swipe left and right to navigate from one picture to another. On Android devices, you swipe down to unlock the phone. On a mobile browser, you can use swipe as well.

Getting ready

First, let's create an HTML document and name it `ch03r04.html`.

How to do it...

1. Enter the following code:

```
<!doctype html>
<html>
  <head>
    <title>Mobile Cookbook</title>
    <meta charset="utf-8">
    <meta name="viewport" content="width=device-width,
initial-scale=1.0">
    <style>
      html, body {
        padding:0;
```

```
      margin:10px auto;
    }
    #checkbox {
      border:5px solid #ccc;
      width:30px;
      height:30px;
    }
    #wrapper {
      width:210px;
      height:100px;
      position:relative;
      overflow:hidden;
      margin:0 auto;
    }
    #inner {
      position:absolute;
      width:630px;
    }
    #inner div {
      width:200px;
      height:100px;
      margin:0 5px;
      background:#ccc;
      float:left;
    }
    .full-circle {
      background-color: #ccc;
      height: 10px;
      -moz-border-radius:5px;
      -webkit-border-radius: 5px;
      width: 10px;
      float:left;
      margin:5px;
    }
    .cur {
      background-color: #555;
    }
    #btns {
      width:60px;
      margin:0 auto;
    }
  </style>
</head>
<body>

  <div id="main">
```

```
    <div id="wrapper">
      <div id="inner">
        <div></div>
        <div></div>
        <div></div>
      </div>
    </div>
    <div id="btns">
      <div class="full-circle cur"></div>
      <div class="full-circle"></div>
      <div class="full-circle"></div>
    </div>
  </div>

  <script src="http://code.jquery.com/jquery-1.5.2.min.js"></
script>
  <script src="http://code.jquery.com/mobile/1.0a4.1/jquery.
mobile-1.0a4.1.min.js"></script>
  <script>
  var curNum = 0;
  $('#wrapper').swipeleft(function () {
    $('#inner').animate({
    left: '-=210'
    }, 500, function() {
      // Animation complete.
      curNum +=1;
      $('.full-circle').removeClass('cur');
      $('.full-circle').eq(curNum).addClass('cur');
    });
  });

  $('#wrapper').swiperight(function () {
    $('#inner').animate({
    left: '+=210'
    }, 500, function() {
      // Animation complete.
      curNum -=1;
      $('.full-circle').removeClass('cur');
      $('.full-circle').eq(curNum).addClass('cur');
    });
  });
  </script>
  </body>
</html>
```

2. Once you've entered the code in the page, swipe left and right of the viewing area, and you can see the boxes being scrolled horizontally:

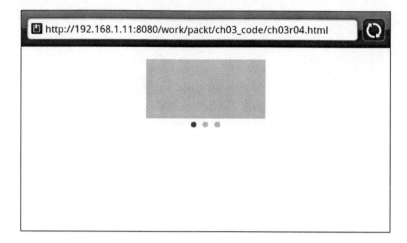

How it works...

We have used a couple of HTML5 techniques in this example. First, we used jQuery Mobile to detect the swipe event. When we use our finger to swipe the page to the left or right, an event listener is assigned:

```
$('#wrapper').swipeleft(function () {
});
$('#wrapper').swiperight(function () {
});
```

When the swipe events are detected, jQuery animation `.animate()` is used to create the moving effect:

```
$('#inner').animate({
    left: '+=210'
    }, 500, function() {
      // Animation complete.
      curNum -=1;
      $('.full-circle').removeClass('cur');
      $('.full-circle').eq(curNum).addClass('cur');
    });
```

There's more...

In this example, we used a CSS3 technique for the circle buttons. You can draw an entire circle using just pure CSS3:

```
.full-circle {
  background-color: #ccc;
  height: 10px;
  -moz-border-radius:5px;
  -webkit-border-radius: 5px;
  border-radius: 5px;
  width: 10px;
}
```

In this example, we define the width and height of the document to be 10 px, and the border radius to be 5 px. Now you can have a perfect circle in just a couple of lines of CSS!

Zepto framework and swipe events

You can use the Zepto framework to do something similar. It has events such as `swipe`, `swipeLeft`, `swipeRight`, `swipeUp`, `swipeDown`.

YUI and gesture events

YUI has gesture events which you can use to create swipe events. You can read more about this here: Supporting A Swipe Left Gesture:

`http://yuiblog.com/sandbox/yui/3.3.0pr3/examples/event/swipe-gesture.html`

Dive into the source

Events in jQuery mobile are built in a modular way. Those who want to learn how jQuery made the swipe event can visit:

`https://github.com/jquery/jquery-mobile/blob/master/js/jquery.mobile.event.js`. The part related to swipe events is under:

```
$.event.special.swipe = {...}
```

Vertical, horizontal, and distance threshold are calculated for the event calculation.

See also

- ▸ *Moving an element with touch events*
- ▸ *Redrawing a canvas with orientation events*
- ▸ *Rotating an HTML element with gesture events*
- ▸ *Zooming an image with gesture events*

Zooming an image with gesture events

On the iPhone, you can resize an element based on zoom detection. On gesture change, you could get the value of the scale factor, and zoom HTML elements based on it.

Getting ready

Create an HTML document and name it ch03r05.html.

How to do it...

Enter the following code:

```
<!doctype html>
<html>
  <head>
    <title>Mobile Cookbook</title>
    <meta charset="utf-8">
    <meta name="viewport" content="width=device-width,
initial-scale=1.0, user-scalable=no">
    <style>
      #frame {
        width:100px;
        height:100px;
        background:#ccc;
      }
    </style>
  </head>
  <body>

    <div id="main">
      <div id="frame"></div>
    </div>

    <script src="http://code.jquery.com/jquery-1.5.2.min.js"></script>
    <script src="http://code.jquery.com/mobile/1.0a4.1/jquery.mobile-
1.0a4.1.min.js"></script>
    <script>
    var width = 100, height = 100;
    var node = document.getElementById('frame');
    node.ongesturechange = function(e){
      var node = e.target;
      // scale and rotation are relative values,
      // so we wait to change our variables until the gesture ends
```

```
        node.style.width = (width * e.scale) + "px";
        node.style.height = (height * e.scale) + "px";
      }
      node.ongestureend = function(e){
        // Update the values for the next time a gesture happens
        width *= e.scale;
        height *= e.scale;
      }
    </script>
  </body>
</html>
```

How it works...

In this example, we assign the element we want to scale with the `ongesturechange` event. The scale factor is determined by the `e.target.scale`:

```
width *= e.scale;
height *= e.scale;
```

There's more...

Gesture events can be tricky, so using them properly is very important. For a two finger multi-touch gesture, the events occur in the following sequence:

1. `touchstart` for finger 1. Sent when the first finger touches the surface.
2. `gesturestart`. Sent when the second finger touches the surface.
3. `touchstart` for finger 2. Sent immediately after `gesturestart` when the second finger touches the surface.
4. `gesturechange` for current gesture. Sent when both fingers move while still touching the surface.
5. `gestureend`. Sent when the second finger lifts from the surface.
6. `touchend` for finger 2. Sent immediately after `gestureend` when the second finger lifts from the surface.
7. `touchend` for finger 1. Sent when the first finger lifts from the surface.

Official iOS Safari guide on GestureEvent

There is an official iPhone Safari guide that explains the details of `GestureEvent` class on Safari:

```
http://developer.apple.com/library/safari/#documentation/
UserExperience/Reference/GestureEventClassReference/GestureEvent/
GestureEvent.html.
```

YUI gesture events

YUI from Yahoo! has a cross-browser solution for gesture events, but only supports one-finger events. You can find out more about it at:

`http://developer.yahoo.com/yui/3/event/#gestures.`

Google Maps and gesture events

One example of a site that relies heavily on the two fingers gesture event is Google Maps on Mobile Safari:

See also

> ▸ *Moving an element with touch events*
>
> ▸ *Redrawing a canvas with orientation events*
>
> ▸ *Rotating an HTML element with gesture events*
>
> ▸ *Making a carousel with swipe events*

4
Building Fast and Responsive Websites

In this chapter, we will cover:

- ▸ Building pages using basic HTML5 markup
- ▸ Using CSS3 features for progressive enhancement
- ▸ Applying responsive design with media query
- ▸ Using dynamic loading
- ▸ Applying user agent detection
- ▸ Adding mobile bookmark bubble to the home page
- ▸ Building Contact page with textarea and autogrow forms
- ▸ Making buttons with instant response
- ▸ Hiding WebKit chrome
- ▸ Building a mobile sitemap

Introduction

On mobile devices, bandwidth is not always as good as on a desktop computer. If you are on a slow 3G network, things can get loaded much slower than on a Wi-Fi hotspot. Even for Wi-Fi connections, many mobile browsers process slower than desktop computers. So when we create mobile sites, they have to be fast and responsive.

From this chapter onwards, we will also start to introduce HTML5 features. HTML5 is a set of technologies consisting of semantics, new CSS rules and properties, and new JavaScript APIs which could be used to build better structured web pages and powerful web applications. The following are the eight main HTML5 features:

- ▸ Semantics
- ▸ Offline and storage
- ▸ Device access
- ▸ Connectivity
- ▸ Multimedia
- ▸ 3D, graphics, and effects
- ▸ Performance and integration
- ▸ CSS3

Not all of these features are mobile exclusive; some are related more to mobile web, while some are more general for both mobile and desktop web. We will talk about each of these features and see how best they could help with our mobile development.

Based on the examples created using the new semantic tags and CSS3, we will discuss many ways to fully leverage what the mobile browser is offering and how to build a website using these unique features.

Building pages using HTML5 semantics

Target device: cross-browser

HTML5 introduced a richer set of tags; these tags give meaning to structure. Semantics is a fundamental aspect of HTML5.

We won't be going through all the tags here, but will cover some of the most commonly used ones.

Getting ready

First, let's create a new HTML file, and name it ch04r01.html. Let's create a fictional site about music.

How to do it...

In our HTML document, type in the following code:

```
<!doctype html>
<html>
  <head>
    <title>first.fm</title>
    <meta charset="utf-8">
    <meta name="viewport" content="width=device-width,
initial-scale=1.0">
    <style>
    </style>
  </head>
  <body>
    <header>
      <h1>first.fm</h1>
    </header>
    <div id="main">
      <h2>Pages</h2>
        <nav>
            <ul>
              <li class="list"><a href="music.html">Music</a></li>
              <li><a href="radio.html">Radio</a></li>
              <li><a href="events.html">Events</a></li>
              <li><a href="charts.html">Charts</a></li>
              <li><a href="community.html">Community</a></li>
              <li><a href="help.html">Help</a></li>
              <li><a href="about.html">About</a></li>
            </ul>
        </nav>
    </div>
    <footer>
      <small>&copy; 2011 first.fm</small>
    </footer>
  </body>
</html>
```

How it works...

The `header` element is often used for h1 to h6 elements; it could appear as the head of the entire page or the head of any block-level element. It often contains a title, subtitle, or tagline.

`<header>` element:

```
<header>
</header>
```

The `nav` element represents navigation for a document. The `nav` element is a section containing links to other documents or to parts within the current document.

Not all groups of links on a page need to be in a `nav` element. It's only groups of primary or secondary navigation links. In particular, it is common for footers to have a list of links to various key parts of a site, but the footer element is more appropriate in such cases.

`<nav>` element:

```
<nav>
  <ul class="list">
    <li class="list"><a href="music.html">Music</a></li>
  </ul>
</nav>
```

The `footer` element represents the "footer" of a document or section of a document. The footer element typically contains metadata about its enclosing section, such as who wrote it, links to related documents, copyright data, and so on. Contact information for the section given in a footer should be marked up using the address element.

`<footer>` element:

```
<footer>
  <small>&copy; 2011 first.fm</small>
</footer>
```

The `small` element can be used for small print. It is not intended to present the main focus of the page. The small element should not be used for lengthy paragraphs or sections of text. It is only intended for short text such as copyright information.

`<small>` element:

```
<small>&copy; 2011 first.fm</small>
```

There's more...

Semantics is more than just a richer set of tags. What we need is more than just more meaningful tags. To extend beyond tags, we could also add extra semantics that are machine-readable; data that browsers, scripts, or robots can understand, enabling a more useful, data-driven web for both programs and your users. These semantics are: **RDFa (Resource Description Framework – in – attributes)**, **Microdata**, and **Microformats**.

RDFa

RDFa provides a set of machine-readable HTML attributes. By using RDFa, authors could turn existing human-readable information into machine-readable data without repeating content. The latest spec can be found at:

```
http://www.w3.org/TR/rdfa-in-html/.
```

Microdata

Microdata uses attributes to define groups of name-value pairs of data. You could learn more about it at: `http://html5doctor.com/microdata/`.

You can dig deeper into microdata by reading the W3C Working Draft at: `http://www.w3.org/TR/microdata/`.

You can also read the W3C Editor's Draft at: `http://dev.w3.org/html5/md/`.

Microformats

Microformats are designed for human's first and machine's second. There are currently 34 microformats specs, some are published, and some are drafts. You can learn more about them at: `http://html5doctor.com/microformats/`.

See also

  ▶   *Using HTML5 on mobile web* in *Chapter 1, HTML5 and the Mobile Web*
  ▶   *Making HTML5 render cross-browser* in *Chapter 1, HTML5 and the Mobile Web*

Using CSS3 features for progressive enhancement

Target device: cross-browser

CSS3 enhances web applications and websites using a wide range of styles and effects. With CSS3, one can create a set of rich UI that is imageless. On mobile, fewer images means faster loading, which is one way to boost performance. With the wide support of CSS3 on most modern smartphone browsers and polyfills for fallback (polyfills are used as fallback to make HTML5 features work on browsers that don't support HTML5 natively), it's not just safe but necessary to start using CSS3!

Getting ready

Let's style the page created in the previous example. First copy `ch04r01.html` and rename it as `ch04r02.html`.

How to do it...

Add in the following style rules:

```
<style>
  body {
    margin:0;
    padding:0;
    font-family:Arial;
    background:#ccc;
  }
  header {
    text-shadow: 0 1px #000;
    background: #ff3019; /* Old browsers */
    background: -moz-linear-gradient(top, #ff3019 0%, #cf0404 20%,
#ff3019 100%); /* FF3.6+ */
    background: -webkit-gradient(linear, left top, left
bottom, color-stop(0%,#ff3019), color-stop(20%,#cf0404), color-
stop(100%,#ff3019)); /* Chrome,Safari4+ */
    background: -webkit-linear-gradient(top, #ff3019 0%,#cf0404
20%,#ff3019 100%); /* Chrome10+,Safari5.1+ */
    background: -o-linear-gradient(top, #ff3019 0%,#cf0404
20%,#ff3019 100%); /* Opera11.10+ */
    background: -ms-linear-gradient(top, #ff3019 0%,#cf0404
20%,#ff3019 100%); /* IE10+ */
    filter: progid:DXImageTransform.Microsoft.gradient(
startColorstr='#ff3019', endColorstr='#ff3019',GradientType=0 ); /*
IE6-9 */
    background: linear-gradient(top, #ff3019 0%,#cf0404 20%,#ff3019
100%); /* W3C */
  }
  h1 {
    padding:0.5em 0.2em;
    margin:0;
    font-size: 18px;
    color:white;
  }
```

```
    h2 {
      text-shadow: 0 1px #FFFFFF;
      background: #eeeeee; /* Old browsers */
      background: -moz-linear-gradient(top, #eeeeee 0%, #cccccc 100%);
/* FF3.6+ */
      background: -webkit-gradient(linear, left top, left bottom,
color-stop(0%,#eeeeee), color-stop(100%,#cccccc)); /* Chrome,Safari4+
*/
      background: -webkit-linear-gradient(top, #eeeeee 0%,#cccccc
100%); /* Chrome10+,Safari5.1+ */
      background: -o-linear-gradient(top, #eeeeee 0%,#cccccc 100%); /*
Opera11.10+ */
      background: -ms-linear-gradient(top, #eeeeee 0%,#cccccc 100%);
/* IE10+ */
      filter: progid:DXImageTransform.Microsoft.gradient(
startColorstr='#eeeeee', endColorstr='#cccccc',GradientType=0 ); /*
IE6-9 */
      background: linear-gradient(top, #eeeeee 0%,#cccccc 100%); /*
W3C */
      padding:0.5em 0.2em;
      margin:0;
      font-size: 16px;
      color:#000;
    }
    nav ul {
      border-top:1px solid #fff;
      list-style-type: none;
      padding:0;
      margin:0;
    }
    nav li {
      padding:0.5em 0.2em;
      margin:0;
      background:#AFAFAF;
      border-bottom:1px solid #fff;
    }
    nav li a {
      height:20px;
      display:block;
      text-decoration:none;
      color:white;
    }
    </style>
```

By running this code in the browser, here is what we can see:

How it works...

In this example, we used CSS3 gradients to style the header element. Traditionally, to create a gradient like the previous example, one would have to use Photoshop or Illustrator, but now you can create it using purely CSS!

```
background: #eeeeee; /* Old browsers */
     background: -moz-linear-gradient(top, #eeeeee 0%, #cccccc 100%);
/* FF3.6+ */
     background: -webkit-gradient(linear, left top, left bottom,
color-stop(0%,#eeeeee), color-stop(100%,#cccccc)); /* Chrome,Safari4+
*/
     background: -webkit-linear-gradient(top, #eeeeee 0%,#cccccc
100%); /* Chrome10+,Safari5.1+ */
     background: -o-linear-gradient(top, #eeeeee 0%,#cccccc 100%); /*
Opera11.10+ */
     background: -ms-linear-gradient(top, #eeeeee 0%,#cccccc 100%);
/* IE10+ */
     filter: progid:DXImageTransform.Microsoft.gradient(
startColorstr='#eeeeee', endColorstr='#cccccc',GradientType=0 ); /*
IE6-9 */
     background: linear-gradient(top, #eeeeee 0%,#cccccc 100%); /*
W3C */
```

By looking at each aforementioned rule, we can see that different browsers use different CSS rules for gradients. There are six different variations just to make sure it's cross-browser compatible. You must be thinking: "Oh, man, it's pretty time consuming to take care of each browser." Don't worry, this rule isn't typed out manually. The **Ultimate CSS Gradient Generator** comes to the rescue! A powerful Photoshop-like CSS gradient editor from ColorZilla can help you make it painless to create CSS3 gradients:

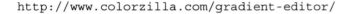

```
http://www.colorzilla.com/gradient-editor/
```

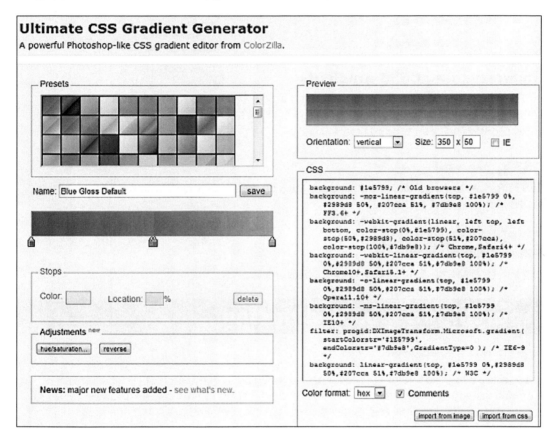

There's more...

If you take IE9 and below into consideration, CSS3 PIE (`http://css3pie.com/`) can be used for support.

After downloading `PIE.htc`, include it in your CSS using:

```
-pie-background: linear-gradient(top, #eeeeee 0%,#cccccc 100%);
/*PIE*/
behavior: url(PIE.htc);
```

Supported features include:

- border-radius

- box-shadow

- border-image

- CSS3 backgrounds (`-pie-background`)

- Gradients

- RGBA color values

- PIE custom properties

Understanding CSS3 gradients

Jeffrey Way, editor at nettuts, has an excellent article about CSS3 gradients. You can view it at: `http://net.tutsplus.com/tutorials/html-css-techniques/quick-tip-understanding-css3-gradients/`.

CSS3, please!

CSS3 Please!, by *Paul Irish*, has the latest syntax on gradients and many other CSS3 features at: `http://css3please.com/`.

See also

- *Using HTML5 on mobile web in Chapter 1*

Applying responsive design

Target device: cross-browser

Responsive design is one of the most important concepts in recent mobile development. It emphasizes the concept that the browser should respond to the screen/browser resize to render differently. A mobile first responsive design could make pages degrade gracefully on desktop browsers.

So why do we need responsive web design?

When we apply fixed layout on a desktop web page, there are often whitespaces on the left or right of the screen depending on the browser screen size. Mobile browsers also come with different sizes, and with limited viewport space, every pixel is vital, so it's important to utilize every pixel available on the screen. To eliminate unnecessary whitespaces on the left or right of the page, responsive design is used.

How could media queries help with responsive design?

Media queries are used to style content based on the screen size update, so for the same HTML element, there could be two separate rules applied. Which one is rendered depends on the size of the browser viewport.

Getting ready

In this example, we will use an HTML5 polyfill named `respond.js`. It is created by *Scott Jehl* (from the jQuery Mobile team). It's located at `ch04_code/js` in the source code.

How to do it...

First, let's create an HTML document named `ch04r03.html`.

Enter the following code in HTML:

```html
<!doctype html>
<html>
  <head>
    <title>first.fm</title>
    <meta charset="utf-8">
    <meta name="viewport" content="width=device-width, initial-scale=1.0">
    <link rel="stylesheet" href="css/style.css?v=1">
    <script>Modernizr.mq('(min-width:0)') || document.write("<script src='js/respond.min.js'>\x3C/script>")</script>
  </head>
  <body>
    <header>
      <h1>first.fm</h1>
    </header>
    <div id="main">
      <h2>Pages</h2>
      <nav>
        <ul class="list clearfix">
          <li class="list"><a href="music.html">Music</a></li>
          <li class="list"><a href="radio.html">Radio</a></li>
          <li class="list"><a href="events.html">Events</a></li>
          <li class="list"><a href="charts.html">Charts</a></li>
          <li class="list"><a href="community.html">Community</a></li>
          <li class="list"><a href="help.html">Help</a></li>
          <li class="list"><a href="about.html">About</a></li>
        </ul>
```

```
      </nav>
    </div>
    <footer>
      <small>&copy; 2011 first.fm</small>
    </footer>
  </body>
</html>
```

If you render the page on a mobile device, this page will look exactly the same as the previous recipe. But if you render it in a desktop browser, it will look similar to the following:

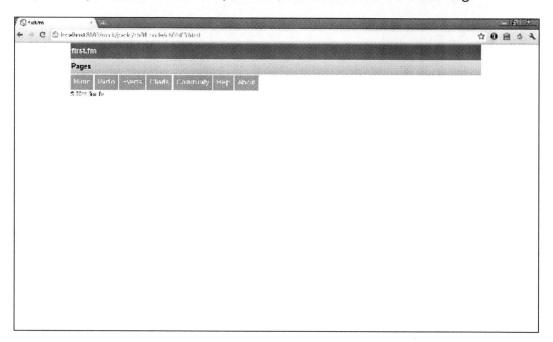

How it works...

At the top of the file, we used **Modernizr** to first detect if Media Queries are supported by the current browser. If not, we will load `respond.min.js`:

```
<script>Modernizr.mq('(min-width:0)') || document.write("<script
src='js/respond.min.js'>\x3C/script>")</script>
```

At the time of writing, you need to have the `/*/mediaquery*/` comment at the end of the rule for it to work. This might be improved in future versions of `respond.js`:

```
@media only screen and (min-width: 800px) {
}/*/mediaquery*/
```

There's more...

On the Mobile Boilerplate site, I have explained further about Media Queries, and you can find the slides at: `http://html5boilerplate.com/mobile/`.

Andy Clarke created *320 and up* which is also based on the idea of responsive design. You can download it at: `http://stuffandnonsense.co.uk/projects/320andup/`.

Optimizing polyfills script loading

Target device: cross-browser

Script loading is important to any browser, but more so for mobile devices because of the low bandwidth. Modernizr comes with a dynamic loading solution.

Getting ready

First, let's create an HTML document and name it `ch03r04.html`.

How to do it...

Enter the following code in your code editor, and run it.

```
<!doctype html>
<html>
  <head>
    <title>first.fm</title>
    <meta charset="utf-8">
    <meta name="viewport" content="width=device-width,
initial-scale=1.0">
    <script src="js/modernizr.custom.54685.js"></script>
    <style>
    </style>
  </head>
```

```
<body>
  <header>
    <h1>Your Location</h1>
  </header>
  <div id="main">
    Your Geo Location is: <span id="geo"></span>
  </div>

  <script src="//ajax.googleapis.com/ajax/libs/jquery/1.5.2/jquery.
js"></script>
  <script>
    yepnope({
      test : Modernizr.geolocation,
      nope : ['js/geolocation.js'],
      complete: function () {           navigator.geolocation.getCurr
entPosition(function(position) {
          document.getElementById('geo').innerHTML = position.
coords.latitude+", "+position.coords.longitude;
        });
      }
    });
  </script>
</body>
</html>
```

How it works...

At the time of writing, Modernizr 2.0 Preview was in Beta 1. In this beta release, there are two great new features. One is that you can choose to customize the features that you want to detect. The other great feature is that you can have yepnope.js (also known as Modernizr.load by *Alex Sexton* and *Ralph Holzmann*). Yepnope.js provides a dynamic JavaScript loader, and you can learn more about it in the *There's more* section of this chapter.

 **BETA 1**
Modernizr 2 Preview

Customize your Modernizr download

Hello! You've landed on the Modernizr 2 beta preview page. Lucky you.

One of the new features we're introducing with Modernizr 2 is the ability to configure your download of Modernizr, so you can limit it to just the tests and features you need and omit the rest. The form below allows you to do this. Please give it a try and tweet us your feedback!

Note:
Whilst this is a Modernizr 2 beta preview, the source code used to put your download together is the 1.7 release.

CSS3   toggle

- [ ] @font-face
- [ ] flexible box model (flexbox)
- [ ] text-shadow
- [ ] rgba()
- [ ] hsla()
- [ ] border-image
- [ ] border-radius
- [ ] box-shadow
- [ ] opacity
- [ ] background-size
- [ ] multiple backgrounds
- [ ] CSS Animations
- [ ] CSS Columns
- [ ] CSS Gradients
- [ ] CSS Reflections
- [ ] CSS 2D Transforms
- [ ] CSS 3D Transforms
- [ ] CSS Transitions

HTML5   toggle

- [ ] applicationCache
- [ ] Canvas
- [ ] Canvas Text
- [ ] Drag 'n Drop
- [ ] hashchange
- [ ] History (pushState)
- [ ] HTML5 Audio
- [ ] HTML5 Video
- [ ] indexedDB
- [ ] Input Types
- [ ] Input Attributes
- [ ] localStorage
- [ ] postMessage
- [ ] sessionStorage
- [ ] Web Workers
- [ ] Web Sockets
- [ ] Web SQL Database

MISC.   toggle

- [ ] Geolocation API
- [ ] Inline SVG
- [ ] SVG
- [ ] SMIL
- [ ] SVG clip paths
- [ ] Touch Events
- [ ] WebGL

OTHER   toggle

- [x] HTML5 Shim/IEPP
- [x] Modernizr.load (yepnope.js)

GENERATE IT!

After generating, copy the source below
or hit the download button

```
// MINIFIED SOURCE
```

With Modernizr, we could first detect if a feature already exists or not in the current user agent:

```
test : Modernizr.geolocation
```

If it doesn't exist, we will load the shim geolocation.js using yepnope. And on completion, we could append the latitude and longitude:

```
yepnope({
  test : Modernizr.geolocation,
    nope : ['js/geolocation.js'],
    complete: function () {
    ...
  });
```

There's more...

There are a couple of optional resources that will be helpful to developers. Modernizr test suite is one of them. It is useful in helping developers know at a glance what features are supported on a certain device. You can find out more at:

```
http://modernizr.github.com/Modernizr/test/index.html.
```

yepnope

yepnope is an asynchronous conditional resource loader that's super-fast and allows you to load only the scripts that your users need. To find out more about it, go to:
`http://yepnopejs.com/`.

See also

  ▸ *Using CSS3 features for progressive enhancement*

Applying user agent detection

Target device: cross-browser

When developing a mobile site, it's good to have user agent detection. This could help you with redirection script or help you to determine if you want to load/not to load something based on user agent.

Getting ready

First, let's see how you could tell if a user could redirect from one site to another based on user agent detection. There are a couple of ways to do this: You could do this in the server config, in your server-side programming language, or use it from the frontend JavaScript.

How to do it...

You can download the redirection script from: `http://detectmobilebrowser.com/`. It comes with many different versions. In this example, let's use the Apache config `.htaccess`.

How it works...

Once you download the file and open it, you will see script as follows:

```
RewriteEngine On
RewriteBase /

RewriteCond %{HTTP_USER_AGENT} android|avantgo|blackberry|blazer|comp
al|
. . . .
|up\.(browser|link)|vodafone|wap|windows\ (ce|phone)|xda|xiino [NC,OR]
RewriteCond %{HTTP_USER_AGENT} ^(1207|6310|6590|
. . . .
|your|zeto|zte\-) [NC]
RewriteRule ^$ http://example.com/mobile [R,L]
```

To redirect a desktop site to a mobile site, one could change the `http://example.com/mobile` to your site address.

There's more...

User agent detection is not only useful for redirecting sites, it's also useful when you are trying to determine if something should be loaded in the first place, based on the user agent.

When building the Mobile Boilerplate site, I used the JavaScript version of the detection script to determine if the site should render the embedded content based on the user agent (mobile or desktop):

```
if(!jQuery.browser.mobile) {
...
}
```

With this script for desktop browsers, the slides are loaded and displayed as follows:

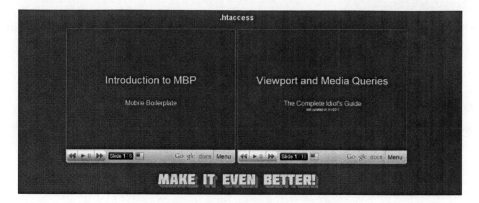

On the mobile version, it is not displayed:

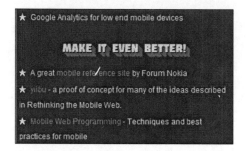

Methods of mobile browser detection

An article on mobile tuts explains different methods of mobile browser detection:
`http://mobile.tutsplus.com/tutorials/mobile-web-apps/mobile-browser-detection/`.

Adding mobile bookmark bubble to the home page

Target device: iOS

In the previous chapters, we have talked about the ability to bookmark your site on certain mobile devices. Although this is a pretty cool feature to bring web apps a step closer to native apps, there is one issue with it: there isn't an API you can use to call the bookmark action, so many users simply are not aware of such a feature on their phone. To tackle this issue, a couple of frameworks provide a bookmark bubble using CSS and JavaScript. The script adds a promo bubble to the bottom of your web app page, asking users to bookmark the web app to their device's home screen.

Getting ready

As mentioned, many frameworks provide this feature, but for simplicity's sake, let's use one that is standalone. Google released an open source library named *The Mobile Bookmark Bubble* for this task. First, let's download it at: `http://code.google.com/p/mobile-bookmark-bubble/`.

How to do it...

The library comes with a `sample.js`. Just include both `bookmark_bubble.js` and the `sample.js` in any webpage created; you would then see something as follows:

How it works...

The library uses HTML5 local storage to track whether the promo has already been displayed, to avoid constantly nagging users. The current implementation of this library specifically targets Mobile Safari, the web browser used on iPhone and iPad devices.

See also

Enabling iPhone start screen in full screen mode in *Chapter 2*

Building Contact page with textarea and autogrow forms

Target device: cross-browser

On native apps like SMS, the textarea grows automatically. On mobile web, if you create a textarea, you will realize it is a fixed size. When the lines of text you type exceed the textarea height, it becomes very hard to see the text. In this example, we will see how we could create a textarea that autogrows when you are typing in more lines.

Getting ready

First, let's create an HTML document and name it `ch04r05.html`. In this example, we will use `helper.js` in Mobile Boilerplate: `https://github.com/h5bp/mobile-boilerplate`

How to do it...

Enter this code in the file:

```
<!doctype html>
<html>
  <head>
    <title>first.fm</title>
    <meta charset="utf-8">
    <meta name="viewport" content="width=device-width, initial-scale=1.0">
    <style>
      #contact {width:220px; height:40px;}
    </style>
  </head>
  <body>
    <header>
      <h1>Contact Form</h1>
    </header>
    <div id="main">
      <p>Type the message to see it autogrow</p>
      <textarea id="contact">
      </textarea>
```

```
    </div>

    <script src="//ajax.googleapis.com/ajax/libs/jquery/1.5.2/jquery.
js"></script>
    <script src="//github.com/shichuan/mobile-html5-boilerplate/raw/
master/js/mylibs/helper.js"></script>
    <script>
      var contact = document.getElementById("contact");
      MBP.autogrow(contact);
    </script>
  </body>
</html>
```

The following is a screenshot of how it renders in Palm webOS:

How it works...

In the script, we have key-up event listener. This will detect if the textarea height has changed. We measure the height of the content and if it's changed, we will change the CSS style of the textarea to increase the height.

There's more...

The original concept is from Google's Code blog. You can read more about it at:
http://googlecode.blogspot.com/2009/07/gmail-for-mobile-html5
-series.html.

See also

▸   *Making buttons with instant response*

Making buttons with instant response

Target device: iOS, Android

On a mobile device browser, button response can be slightly slower than on a native application. On mobile browsers, there is a `touchstart` event. By detecting this event instead of the click event, it will make the clicking faster.

Getting ready

In this example, we will use a function in Mobile Boilerplate. Create a file called `ch04r06.html`.

How to do it...

The following code will create a form with a submit button:

```
<!doctype html>
<html>
  <head>
    <title>first.fm</title>
    <meta charset="utf-8">
    <meta name="viewport" content="width=device-width,
initial-scale=1.0">
    <style>
      #contact {
        width:220px; height:40px;
      }
    </style>
  </head>
  <body>
    <header>
      <h1>Contact Form</h1>
    </header>
    <div id="main">
      <textarea id="contact"></textarea><br />
      <button id="btn">INSTANT button!!!</button><br />
      <span id="result"></span>
    </div>
```

```
    <footer>
      <small>&copy; 2011 first.fm</small>
    </footer>
    <script src="//ajax.googleapis.com/ajax/libs/jquery/1.5.1/jquery.
js"></script>
    <script src="//github.com/shichuan/mobile-html5-boilerplate/raw/
master/js/mylibs/helper.js"></script>
    <script>
      var btn = document.getElementById("btn");
      MBP.fastButton(btn,showForm);
      function showForm() {
        $("#result").html("Thank you for submitting, we will get back
to you shortly!");
      }
    </script>
  </body>
</html>
```

How it works...

The following is the excerpt of the fast button function, and here we will see how the function works.

At the top, we have the main function defined. This is only used if `addEventListener` is supported, where it listens to `touchstart` and `click` events:

```
MBP.fastButton = function (element, handler) {
    this.element = element;
    this.handler = handler;
    if (element.addEventListener) {
      element.addEventListener('touchstart', this, false);
      element.addEventListener('click', this, false);
    }
};

MBP.fastButton.prototype.handleEvent = function(event) {
    switch (event.type) {
        case 'touchstart': this.onTouchStart(event); break;
        case 'touchmove': this.onTouchMove(event); break;
        case 'touchend': this.onClick(event); break;
        case 'click': this.onClick(event); break;
    }
};
```

The onTouchStart method is used to listen to touchmove and touchend events. stopPropagation is used to stop the propagation of the event in the listeners, so that it stops bubbling up:

```
MBP.fastButton.prototype.onTouchStart = function(event) {
    event.stopPropagation();
    this.element.addEventListener('touchend', this, false);
    document.body.addEventListener('touchmove', this, false);
    this.startX = event.touches[0].clientX;
    this.startY = event.touches[0].clientY;
    this.element.style.backgroundColor = "rgba(0,0,0,.7)";
};
```

touchmove is used to test if the user is dragging. If users drag past 10 px, we will reset it:

```
MBP.fastButton.prototype.onTouchMove = function(event) {
    if(Math.abs(event.touches[0].clientX - this.startX) > 10 || Math.abs(event.touches[0].clientY - this.startY) > 10) {
        this.reset();
    }
};
```

The following code prevents ghost clicks and invokes the actual click handler:

```
MBP.fastButton.prototype.onClick = function(event) {
    event.stopPropagation();
    this.reset();
    this.handler(event);
    if(event.type == 'touchend') {
        MBP.preventGhostClick(this.startX, this.startY);
    }
    this.element.style.backgroundColor = "";
};
```

```
MBP.fastButton.prototype.reset = function() {
    this.element.removeEventListener('touchend', this, false);
    document.body.removeEventListener('touchmove', this, false);
    this.element.style.backgroundColor = "";
};
```

There's more...

You can read more about fast button at Google's blog. It explains in detail the background and theory behind the idea at: http://code.google.com/mobile/articles/fast_buttons.html.

Building Contact page with textarea and autogrow forms

Hiding WebKit chrome

Target device: iOS, Android

The URL bar at the top of mobile Safari on iOS and Android uses a large space. Many developers will hide it on page load as mobile real estate is limited. Every pixel is important and, by hiding the URL bar, it helps you to leverage every pixel on the screen to maximize the display area.

Getting ready

First, let's create an HTML document and name it `ch04r07.html`.

How to do it...

Enter this code:

```
<!doctype html>
<html>
  <head>
    <title>Mobile Cookbook</title>
    <meta charset="utf-8">
    <meta name="viewport" content="width=device-width,
initial-scale=1.0">
    <style>
      html,body,header,footer{
        padding:0;
        margin:0;
      }
      header{
        height:40px;
        background:#BFB840;
        display:block;
      }
      #main{
        height:350px;
        background:#F2CB67;
      }
```

```
        footer{
          height:40px;
          background:#DB5E31;
          display:block;
        }
    </style>
  </head>
  <body>
    <header>
      header
    </header>
    <div id="main">
      main
    </div>
    <footer>
      footer
    </footer>
    <script src="//ajax.googleapis.com/ajax/libs/jquery/1.5.1/jquery.
js"></script>
    <script src="//github.com/shichuan/mobile-html5-boilerplate/raw/
master/js/mylibs/helper.js"></script>
    <script>
      //MBP.hideUrlBar();
    </script>
  </body>
</html>
```

Now if you render it in the browser, it will look like this:

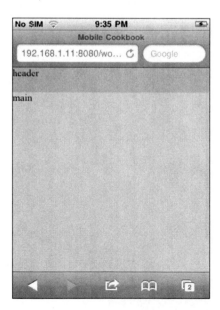

Now uncomment the following line:

```
MBP.hideUrlBar();
```

Render the content again and you can see the chrome is now hidden, allowing the footer to display:

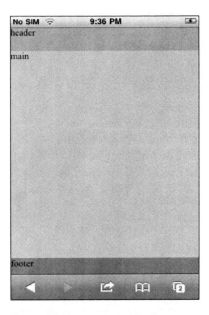

How it works...

The following is the script inside Boilerplate:

```
MBP.hideUrlBar = function () {
  var win = window,
    doc = win.document;

  // If there's a hash, or addEventListener is undefined, stop here
  if( !location.hash || !win.addEventListener ){

    //scroll to 1
    window.scrollTo( 0, 1 );
    var scrollTop = 1,

    //reset to 0 on bodyready, if needed
    bodycheck = setInterval(function(){
      if( doc.body ){
        clearInterval( bodycheck );
        scrollTop = "scrollTop" in doc.body ? doc.body.scrollTop : 1;
```

```
            win.scrollTo( 0, scrollTop === 1 ? 0 : 1 );
        }
    }, 15 );

    win.addEventListener( "load", function(){
        setTimeout(function(){
            //reset to hide addr bar at onload
            win.scrollTo( 0, scrollTop === 1 ? 0 : 1 );
        }, 0);
    }, false );
    }
};
```

It detects if there is any hash in the URL. If there is, we will stop running the script because it means there is an inline anchor. If there isn't any hash, we will wait for a second and if there isn't scrolling, Android uses 1 px y pos for hiding, while it's 0 in iOS. The script normalizes the two. It's made by *Scott Jehl* at: `https://gist.github.com/1183357`.

It's also included in Mobile Boilerplate at: `https://github.com/h5bp/mobile-boilerplate/blob/master/js/mylibs/helper.js`.

See also

Building Contact page with textarea and autogrow forms

Building a mobile sitemap

Target device: cross-browser

Many developers are familiar with Google Sitemap. As the biggest search engine, making sure it gets our content is very important. For mobile SEO purposes, Google came up with **Mobile Sitemap**. Google recommends that people update their mobile sitemaps to the format described next.

Getting ready

First, let's create an XML document and name it `sitemap.xml`.

How to do it...

We can add the following code to the XML document. For the particular site you have, the URL should be the URL of your pages:

```
<?xml version="1.0" encoding="UTF-8" ?>
 <urlset xmlns="http://www.sitemaps.org/schemas/sitemap/0.9"
  xmlns:mobile="http://www.google.com/schemas/sitemap-mobile/1.0">
    <url>
        <loc>http://mobile.example.com/article100.html</loc>
        <mobile:mobile/>
    </url>
</urlset>
```

All the URLs are enclosed inside `<loc></loc>`.

Make sure you have included `<mobile:mobile/>`. Otherwise, sites will not be properly crawled.

How it works...

Sitemaps follow a particular schema; the aforementioned XML schema is used to tell Google search engine the location of the mobile web page. Normally, if a site is built using a CMS system, there should be a way to auto-generate the URLs, and they should all be listed within `<loc></loc>`.

There's more...

Mobile sitemap cannot contain desktop-only URLs. However, it can contain content for both desktop and mobile.

For websites with dedicated mobile content and a dedicated URL, you may direct users from `example.com` to `m.example.com`. In this case, use a 301 redirect for both users and Googlebot-Mobile.

If you serve all types of content from `example.com`, this is not considered cloaking by Google.

Google and mobile-friendly site building

On the Google Webmaster site, there is a blog post about how to make websites mobile friendly: `http://googlewebmastercentral.blogspot.com/2011/02/making-websites-mobile-friendly.html`.

Google and mobile site indexing

There is another blog on Google Webmaster site, which talks about how to help Google index your mobile site: `http://googlewebmastercentral.blogspot.com/2009/11/help-google-index-your-mobile-site.html`.

5
Mobile Device Access

In this chapter, we will cover:

- ► Getting your location
- ► Handling cross-browser geolocation
- ► Displaying a map based on your geolocation
- ► Realtime positioning
- ► `DeviceOrientation` event
- ► Using geolocation with foursquare

Introduction

Among all the HTML5 classes, one that is most closely related to mobile development has to be Device Access.

Here is the official description of Device Access on the W3C HTML5 Movement site (`http://www.w3.org/html/logo/`):

> Beginning with the Geolocation API, Web Applications can present rich, device-aware features, and experiences. Incredible device access innovations are being developed and implemented, from audio/video input access to microphones and cameras, to local data such as contacts and events, and even tilt orientation.

You can find the description and logo at: `http://www.w3.org/html/logo/#the-technology`.

Location-based social networks like foursquare have had a profound impact on the way business works and how people mobilize. Groupon's new location-based offer, if it's released, may fundamentally change consumer behavior and the way retail businesses function. Google Maps uses realtime geolocation and GPRS to help people and vehicles navigate. There will be more and more exciting innovations built on top of this Device Access technology.

In this chapter, we will study geolocation API and DeviceOrientation API, address cross-browser issues, and see how we can use Device Access together with popular location-based services.

Getting your location

Target browsers: Android, iOS, webOS, Opera, Firefox

Using the geolocation API, we could return values like latitude, longitude, and accuracy of your current location:

▸ Latitude and longitude: These attributes are geographic coordinates and are specified in decimal degrees

▸ Accuracy: Denotes the accuracy level of the latitude and longitude coordinates and is specified in meters

Getting ready

Let's create an HTML document and get the latitude and longitude together with the accuracy. First, let's create a new HTML file, and name it ch05r01.html.

How to do it...

Enter the following code into the HTML document:

```
<!doctype html>
<html>
  <head>
    <title>Mobile Cookbook</title>
    <meta charset="utf-8">
    <meta name="viewport" content="width=device-width,
initial-scale=1.0">
  </head>
  <body>

    <div id="main">
            <div id="someElm">
            </div>
    </div>
```

```
    <script src="http://code.jquery.com/jquery-1.5.2.min.js"></script>
    <script>
    function getLocation() {
     navigator.geolocation.getCurrentPosition(showInfo);
    }
  function showInfo(position) {
    var latitude = position.coords.latitude;
    var longitude = position.coords.longitude;
    var accuracy = position.coords.accuracy;
    $('#someElm').html('latitude: '+latitude+'<br />longitude:
'+longitude+'<br />accuracy: '+accuracy);
  }
  getLocation();
    </script>
    </body>
</html>
```

When you first render it, you will be prompted with a message as follows:

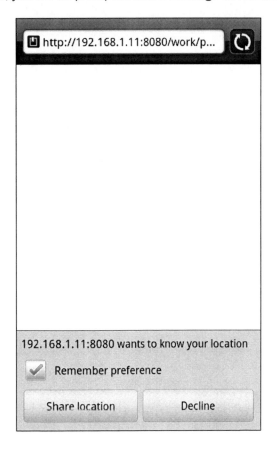

Geolocation support is opt-in. No browser will automatically send the physical location of your device to the server. Instead, it will ask for your permission before executing the program of sending the location of your device back and forth. The browser can remember your preference to prevent it from popping up again from the same site.

Now press the button that allows you to share the location. You will then get the location data displayed on the screen as follows:

How it works...

navigator is an object that is no stranger to JavaScript programmers. It's commonly used for user agent detection: navigator.userAgent.

geolocation is a new property on the navigator object: navigator.geolocation.

getCurrentPosition is a method of navigator.geolocation. In this example, we execute the function showInfo as the first argument:

```
navigator.geolocation.getCurrentPosition(showInfo);
```

In the showInfo function, we return three values from position parameter, that is, latitude, longitude, and accuracy:

```
var latitude = position.coords.latitude;
var longitude = position.coords.longitude;
var accuracy = position.coords.accuracy;
```

There's more...

So, are the aforementioned attributes all that the geolocation API could return? Theoretically, more information can be returned, but in reality, only selected browsers will return additional information.

Handling cross-browser geolocation

Target browsers: cross-browser

Geolocation doesn't work on all mobile browsers, and even for those browsers that do support it, they could have an API that's different from the standard. iOS and Android use the standard. Browsers that are known to have a different API include Blackberry, Nokia, and Palm. Luckily, we have a mobile-centric geolocation polyfill – **geo-location-javascript**. It has non-standard Blackberry and webOS tricks to help normalize different API behaviors.

Getting ready

Download the resources that come with this chapter and create a js folder. Put geo.js into the js folder. Now create an HTML document named ch05r02.html.

How to do it...

Enter the following code into the HTML document:

```
<!doctype html>
<html>
<head>
<title>Mobile Cookbook</title>
<meta charset="utf-8">
<meta name="viewport" content="width=device-width, initial-scale=1.0">
<script src="http://code.google.com/apis/gears/gears_init.js"
type="text/javascript" charset="utf-8"></script>
<script src="js/geo.js" type="text/javascript" charset="utf-8"></
script>
</head>
<body>

  <div id="main">
    <div id="someElm">
          </div>
  </div>
```

```
<script src="http://code.jquery.com/jquery-1.5.2.min.js"></script>
<script>
  if(geo_position_js.init()){
    geo_position_js.getCurrentPosition(success_callback,error_callba
ck,{enableHighAccuracy:true,options:5000});
  }
  else{
    $('#someElm').html("Functionality not available");
  }
  function success_callback(p)
  {
    $('#someElm').html('latitude: '+p.coords.latitude+'<br
/>longitude: '+p.coords.longitude+'<br />accuracy: '+p.coords.
accuracy);
  }
  function error_callback(p)
  {
    $('#someElm').html('error='+p.message);
  }
</script>
</body>
</html>
```

Test it in Opera and you should be able to see the result as follows:

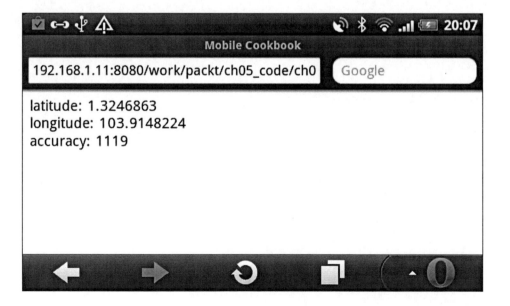

How it works...

At the top of the HTML document, we link to `gears_init.js`. If the browser doesn't have a geolocation API supported by default, but has Gears installed, the Gears API may return the geolocation data. For browsers that have the geolocation API, but just in a different method, the second script `geo.js` will be used to normalize the API.

If `geo_position_js.init()` returns true, it means in one way or anther we are able to get the geolocation data. In this case we will proceed to the next step. Instead of using `navigator.geolocation.getCurrentPosition`, we use `geo_position_js.getCurrentPosition` as the method:

```
geo_position_js.getCurrentPosition(showInfo,error_callback,{enableHigh
Accuracy:true,options:5000});
```

There's more...

Here is an additional resource that will help you to get geolocation info.

YQL Geo Library

YQL Geo Library provides an alternative approach, an IP address-based geolocation. It is a lightweight library that is tied to Yahoo services. It can:

 ▸ Get the geographical location from a text
 ▸ Get the location information from lat/lon
 ▸ Get all the geographical locations from a certain URL
 ▸ Get the place from an IP number

Displaying a map based on your geolocation

Target browsers: cross-browser

The Google Maps API V3 has been designed to load fast and work well on mobile devices. In particular, we have focused on development for advanced mobile devices such as the iPhone and handsets running the Android operating system. Mobile devices have smaller screen sizes than typical browsers on the desktop. As well, they often have particular behavior specific to those devices, such as "pinch-to-zoom" on the iPhone.

Getting ready

Let's create a map that displays on your mobile device. First, let's create an HTML document named `ch05r03.html`.

How to do it...

Enter the following code:

```html
<!doctype html>
<html>
<head>
<title>Mobile Cookbook</title>
<meta charset="utf-8">
<meta name="viewport" content="initial-scale=1.0, user-scalable=no" />
<script type="text/javascript" src="http://maps.google.com/maps/api/
js?sensor=true"></script>
<script src="http://code.google.com/apis/gears/gears_init.js"></
script>
<script src="js/geo.js"></script>
<style>
html {
  height: auto;
}
body {
  height: auto;
  margin: 0;
  padding: 0;
}
#map_canvas {
  height: auto;
  position: absolute;
  bottom:0;
  left:0;
  right:0;
  top:0;
}
</style>
</head>
<body>
  <div id="map_canvas"></div>
  <script src="http://code.jquery.com/jquery-1.5.2.min.js"></script>
  <script>
    var initialLocation;
    var siberia = new google.maps.LatLng(60, 105);
    var newyork = new google.maps.LatLng(40.69847032728747,
-73.9514422416687);
    var browserSupportFlag =  new Boolean();
    var map;
```

```
    var infowindow = new google.maps.InfoWindow();

    function initialize() {
      var myOptions = {
        zoom: 12,
        mapTypeId: google.maps.MapTypeId.ROADMAP
      };
      map = new google.maps.Map(document.getElementById("map_canvas"),
myOptions);

      if(geo_position_js.init()){
        browserSupportFlag = true;
        geo_position_js.getCurrentPosition(function(position) {
          initialLocation = new google.maps.LatLng(position.coords.
latitude,position.coords.longitude);
          contentString = "you are here";
          map.setCenter(initialLocation);
          infowindow.setContent(contentString);
          infowindow.setPosition(initialLocation);
          infowindow.open(map);
        });
      }
    }

    function detectBrowser() {
      var useragent = navigator.userAgent;
      var mapdiv = document.getElementById("map_canvas");

      if (useragent.indexOf('iPhone') != -1 || useragent.
indexOf('Android') != -1) {
        mapdiv.style.width = '100%';
        mapdiv.style.height = '100%';
      } else {
        mapdiv.style.width = '600px';
        mapdiv.style.height = '800px';
      }
    }
    detectBrowser();
    initialize();
  </script>
</body>
</html>
```

When rendered in your mobile browser, it looks as follows:

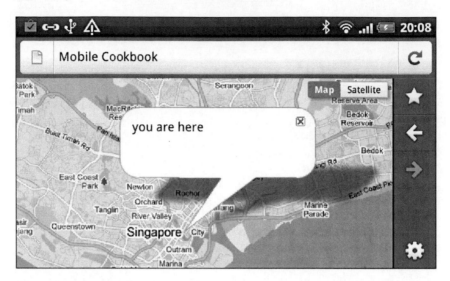

How it works...

Now let's break down the code and see what each section does:

1. The iPhone has the pinch-to-zoom feature and Google Maps API V3 has special handling for this event. So you can set the following metatag and this will make sure that the users cannot resize the iPhone. Android devices running software version 1.5 (Cupcake) also support these parameters:

    ```
    <meta name="viewport" content="initial-scale=1.0, user-scalable=no" />
    ```

2. Set the `<div>` containing your map to have width and height attributes of 100 percent:

    ```
    mapdiv.style.width = '100%';
    mapdiv.style.height = '100%';
    ```

3. You can detect iPhone and Android devices by inspecting the `navigator.userAgent` property within the DOM:

    ```
    function detectBrowser() {
      var useragent = navigator.userAgent;
      var mapdiv = document.getElementById("map_canvas");

      if (useragent.indexOf('iPhone') != -1 || useragent.indexOf('Android') != -1 ) {
        mapdiv.style.width = '100%';
    ```

```
        mapdiv.style.height = '100%';
    } else {
        mapdiv.style.width = '600px';
        mapdiv.style.height = '800px';
    }
}
```

4. Specifying the Sensor Parameter, applications that determine the user's location using a sensor must pass `sensor=true` when loading the Maps API JavaScript.

    ```
    <script type="text/javascript" src="http://maps.google.com/maps/
    api/js?sensor=true"></script>
    ```

    Use of the Google Maps API requires that you indicate whether your application is using a sensor (such as a GPS locator) to determine the user's location. This is especially important for mobile devices. Applications must pass a required sensor parameter to the `<script>` tag when including the Maps API JavaScript code, indicating whether or not your application is using a sensor device.

> Note that even if we are targeting a device that does not use a sensing device, we must still pass this parameter, setting its value to `false`.

5. We parse in the geolocation coordinates to the map API's `LatLng` method:

    ```
    initialLocation = new google.maps.LatLng(position.coords.
    latitude,position.coords.longitude);
    ```

There's more...

You can learn more about Google Maps JavaScript API V3 at the official documentation page at:

```
http://code.google.com/apis/maps/documentation/javascript/
```

HTML5 geolocation tutorial

Mobile tuts has an excellent article about mobile geolocation called *HTML5 Apps: Positioning with Geolocation*. You can read it at:

HTML5 Apps: Positioning with Geolocation

```
http://mobile.tutsplus.com/tutorials/mobile-web-apps/html5-
geolocation/
```

Displaying location in realtime

Target browsers: cross-browser

Apart from `getCurrentPosition`, geolocation API has another method named `watchPosition`. It performs two important actions when called:

1. It returns a value that identifies a watch operation.
2. It asynchronously starts the watch operation.

Getting ready

Let's create an HTML document and name it `ch05r04.html`.

How to do it...

Enter the following code into the document:

```
<!doctype html>
<html>
<head>
<title>Mobile Cookbook</title>
<meta charset="utf-8">
<meta name="viewport" content="initial-scale=1.0, user-scalable=no" />
<style>
html {
  height: auto;
}
body {
  height: auto;
  margin: 0;
  padding: 0;
}
#map_canvas {
  height: auto;
  position: absolute;
  bottom:0;
  left:0;
  right:0;
  top:0;
}
</style>
</head>
```

```
<body>
<div id="map_canvas"></div>
<script type="text/javascript" src="http://maps.google.com/maps/api/
js?sensor=true"></script>
<script src="http://code.jquery.com/jquery-1.5.2.min.js"></script>
<script>
var watchProcess = null;
var initialLocation;
var map;
var infowindow = new google.maps.InfoWindow();
var myOptions = {
  zoom: 12,
  mapTypeId: google.maps.MapTypeId.ROADMAP
};

map = new google.maps.Map(document.getElementById("map_canvas"),
myOptions);

navigator.geolocation.getCurrentPosition(function(position) {
  updatePos(position.coords.latitude,position.coords.
longitude,position.coords.accuracy);
});

initiate_watchlocation();

function initiate_watchlocation() {
  if (watchProcess == null) {
    watchProcess = navigator.geolocation.watchPosition(handle_
geolocation_query, handle_errors);
  }
}

function stop_watchlocation() {
  if (watchProcess != null)
  {
    navigator.geolocation.clearWatch(watchProcess);
    watchProcess = null;
  }
}

function handle_errors(error)
{
  switch(error.code)
```

```
    {
    case error.PERMISSION_DENIED: alert("user did not share geolocation
data");
      break;

    case error.POSITION_UNAVAILABLE: alert("could not detect current
position");
      break;

    case error.TIMEOUT: alert("retrieving position timedout");
      break;

    default: alert("unknown error");
      break;
    }
}

function handle_geolocation_query(position) {
  updatePos(position.coords.latitude,position.coords.
longitude,position.coords.accuracy);
}

function updatePos(lat,long,acc) {
  var text = "Latitude: "  + lat  + "<br/>" + "Longitude: " + long +
"<br/>" + "Accuracy: "  + acc  + "m<br/>";
  initialLocation = new google.maps.LatLng(lat,long);
  contentString = text;
  map.setCenter(initialLocation);
  infowindow.setContent(contentString);
  infowindow.setPosition(initialLocation);
  infowindow.open(map);
}
</script>
</body>
</html>
```

Here is how it will be rendered:

How it works...

The following function will initiate the location watch:

```
function initiate_watchlocation() {
  if (watchProcess == null) {
    watchProcess = navigator.geolocation.watchPosition(handle_
geolocation_query, handle_errors);
  }
}
```

navigator.geolocation.watchPosition will either return success or error upon execution. In the success function, you can parse the latitude and longitude:

```
navigator.geolocation.watchPosition(handle_geolocation_query,
handle_errors);
```

When the position is being watched, the `handle_geolocation_query` is used to get the current position and parse to the update position function:

```
function handle_geolocation_query(position) {
   updatePos(position.coords.latitude,position.coords.
longitude,position.coords.accuracy);
}
```

Using the DeviceOrientation event

Target browsers: iOS

The `DeviceOrientation` event is an important aspect of Device Access. It includes device motion events and device orientation events. Unfortunately, these events are currently supported in iOS only.

Getting ready

Create an HTML document and name it `ch05r05.html`.

How to do it...

Enter the following code into the document:

```
<!doctype html>
<html>
<head>
<title>Mobile Cookbook</title>
<meta charset="utf-8">
<meta name="viewport" content="initial-scale=1.0, user-scalable=no" />
<script type="text/javascript" src="http://maps.google.com/maps/api/
js?sensor=true"></script>
<style>
#no {
    display: none;
}
#ball {
    width: 20px;
    height: 20px;
    border-radius: 10px;

    background-color: red;
    position:absolute;
    top: 0px;
    left: 0px;
}
```

```
</style>
</head>
<body>
  <div id="content">
    <h1>Move the Ball</h1>
    <div id="yes">
        <p>Move your device to move the ball.</p>
        <div id="ball"></div>
    </div>
    <div id="no">
    Your browser does not support Device Orientation and Motion API.
Try this sample with iPhone, iPod or iPad with iOS 4.2+.</div>
  </div>
  <script>
  // Position Variables
  var x = 0;
  var y = 0;

  // Speed - Velocity
  var vx = 0;
  var vy = 0;

  // Acceleration
  var ax = 0;
  var ay = 0;

  var delay = 10;
  var vMultiplier = 0.01;

  if (window.DeviceMotionEvent==undefined) {
    document.getElementById("no").style.display="block";
    document.getElementById("yes").style.display="none";

  } else {
    window.ondevicemotion = function(event) {
      ax = event.accelerationIncludingGravity.x;
      ay = event.accelerationIncludingGravity.y;
    }

    setInterval(function() {
      vy = vy + -(ay);
      vx = vx + ax;

      var ball = document.getElementById("ball");
      y = parseInt(y + vy * vMultiplier);
      x = parseInt(x + vx * vMultiplier);

      if (x<0) { x = 0; vx = 0; }
      if (y<0) { y = 0; vy = 0; }
      if (x>document.documentElement.clientWidth-20) { x = document.
```

```
documentElement.clientWidth-20; vx = 0; }
    if (y>document.documentElement.clientHeight-20) { y = document.
documentElement.clientHeight-20; vy = 0; }

    ball.style.top = y + "px";
    ball.style.left = x + "px";
  }, delay);
}
</script>
</body>
</html>
```

How it works...

This code was made by *Maximiliano Firtman* (http://www.mobilexweb.com/blog/
safari-ios-accelerometer-websockets-html5). In the example, we used
accelerationIncludingGravity. It returns the value of the total acceleration of the
device, which includes the user acceleration and the gravity.

The three values, x, y, z, represent the acceleration in m/s^2 for each axis:

```
window.ondevicemotion = function(event) {
  event.accelerationIncludingGravity.x
  event.accelerationIncludingGravity.y
  event.accelerationIncludingGravity.z
}
```

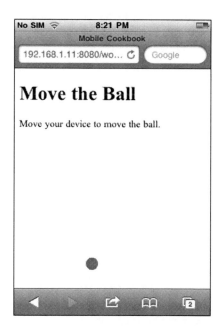

There's more...

Here is a table that shows the current support for `DeviceOrientationEvent` and `DeviceMotionEvent`:

Properties	Description	Returned values	Class	Support
acceleration	*The acceleration that the user is giving to the device.*	*x, y, z (in m/ s^2)*	DeviceMotion Event	*iPhone 4 / iPod Touch 4G*
acceleration IncludingGravity	*The total acceleration of the device, which includes the user acceleration and the gravity.*	*x, y, z (in m/ s^2)*	DeviceMotion Event	*iPhone3 / iPod Touch 3G*
interval	*The interval in milliseconds since the last device motion event.*	*milliseconds*	DeviceMotion Event	*iPhone3 / iPod Touch 3G*
rotationRate	*The rotation rate of the device.*	*alpha, beta, and gamma (values are between 0 and 360)*	DeviceMotionEvent	*iPhone 4 / iPod Touch 4G*
alpha	*The degrees the device frame is rotated around its z-axis.*	*Values are between 0 and 360.*	DeviceOrientation Event	*iPhone 4 / iPod Touch 4G*

Properties	Description	Returned values	Class	Support
`beta`	*The degrees the device frame is rotated around its x-axis.*	*Values are between -180 and 180.*	`DeviceOrientation Event`	*iPhone 4 / iPod Touch 4G*
`gamma`	*The degrees the device frame is rotated around its y-axis.*	*Values are between -90 and 90.*	`DeviceOrientation Event`	*iPhone 4 / iPod Touch 4G*

DeviceOrientation event specification

`http://dev.w3.org/geo/api/spec-source-orientation.html`

Offical guide on the Safari site

`DeviceOrientation` event specification:

`https://developer.apple.com/library/safari/#documentation/`
`SafariDOMAdditions/Reference/DeviceMotionEventClassRef/`
`DeviceMotionEvent/DeviceMotionEvent.html`

`DeviceOrientationEvent` class reference:

`https://developer.apple.com/library/safari/#documentation/`
`SafariDOMAdditions/Reference/DeviceOrientationEventClassRef/`
`DeviceOrientationEvent/DeviceOrientationEvent.html`

Using geolocation with foursquare

Target browsers: cross-browser

In recent years, the location-based social networking website foursquare has become more and more popular. It affected the way many business work and consumers behave. Users "check-in" at places using a mobile website, mobile app, or SMS.

Getting ready

Third-party developers have released many libraries for accessing the foursquare API from various programming languages. One of those is Marelle. It's based on jQuery and written in coffeescript. Don't worry, that's just JavaScript.

How to do it...

Go to the GitHub page of Marelle (`http://praized.github.com/marelle/`) and download the latest version. There are two examples, one is login and another is check-in.

Here is what the login script looks like:

```
// Supply your foursquare client id
var FSQUARE_CLIENT_ID = 'FOURSQUARE_CLIENT_ID';
// on DOM ready...
$(function() {
  // setup with your key and a callback function which
  // receives the Marelle Object ( "M" in this example )
  $.Marelle( FSQUARE_CLIENT_ID ).done( function( M ){
    // grab an authentication promise
    var authpromise = M.authenticateVisitor();
    //  handle logged-in visitor
    var authsuccess = function(visitor){
      M.signoutButton( document.body );
      console.log(visitor)
      /*
      I think the single entry point is through the visitor
      */
      venuepromise = visitor.getVenues()
      // venuepromise.then etc..etc...
    };
    // handle non visitor
    var authfailure = function() {
      M.signinButton( document.body );
    };
    // wait for promise to resolve
    authpromise.then(authsuccess,authfailure)

  }).fail(function(){
    consoloe.log('Marelle could not be loaded.')
  });
});
```

How it works...

Here's how it works:

1. First we trigger Marelle initialization $.Marelle(clientID) and it returns a promise:

   ```
   $.Marelle( FSQUARE_CLIENT_ID )
   ```

2. Then we grab an authentication promise using $.Marelle.authenticateVisitor():

   ```
   $.Marelle( FSQUARE_CLIENT_ID ).done( function( M ){
       var authpromise = M.authenticateVisitor();
   });
   ```

3. Depending on the result of the authentication, authpromise.then() is used to either execute authsuccess or authfailure:

   ```
   authpromise.then(authsuccess,authfailure)
   ```

4. If the authentication is successful, it appends a "disconnect" button to the provided selector:

   ```
   M.signoutButton( document.body );
   ```

5. One can return a list of recommended venues, add or search venues:

   ```
   venuepromise = visitor.getVenues()
   ```

6. If the authentication is unsuccessful, it appends a "Connect" button to the provided selector:

   ```
   M.signinButton( document.body );
   ```

There's more..

A list of foursquare APIs can be found at:

```
https://developer.foursquare.com/docs/libraries.html
```

6
Mobile Rich Media

In this chapter, we will cover:

- ▸ Playing audio from a mobile browser
- ▸ Streaming video on the go
- ▸ Using Appcache for offline viewing
- ▸ Using Web Storage for feed or e-mail applications
- ▸ Using web workers for heavy computation work
- ▸ Creating Flash-like navigation with session and history API

Introduction

With HTML5, you can build rich media applications to display for mobile devices. There are unlimited ways to use HTML5; the only limit is one's imagination.

In the previous chapters, we have covered semantic naming, CSS3, and Device Access categories of HTML5. In this chapter, we will go through three more categories:

- ▸ **Multimedia** – More and more people are playing video and audio on the go, we will see how to embed these elements on mobile devices.
- ▸ **Offline and Storage** – Offline is an important feature for mobile as the connectivity isn't consistent on a mobile device. Storage is useful for mobile to store data on the device to reduce fetching each time the user revisits the page.
- ▸ **Performance and Integration** – With support of web workers on iOS and Blackberry, we could achieve better performance on mobile browsers.

Playing audio on mobile

Target browsers: iOS, Android, Blackberry, webOS, Opera Mobile, Firefox Mobile

Multimedia consists of audio and video. Playing audio on mobile can be tricky. There are a few supported audio formats on mobile browsers – Ogg Vorbis, MP3, and WAV. One issue with these formats is that all of them are not supported by all browsers.

Getting ready

Create an HTML document and name it ch06r01.html.

How to do it...

Enter the following code in the document:

```
<!doctype html>
<html>
  <head>
    <title>Mobile Cookbook</title>
    <meta charset="utf-8">
    <meta name="viewport" content="width=device-width, initial-
scale=1.0">
  </head>
  <body>

    <div id="main">
       <audio src="resources/snake_charmer.mp3" controls preload="auto"
autobuffer>
       </audio>
    </div>

  </body>
</html>
```

Now when rendering it in the browser, you will see a music player displayed as follows, and when you press play, the music should stream:

How it works...

Using the audio tag is fairly simple. The audio is enclosed in the `<audio></audio>` tags.

`controls` tells the audio element to show visual controls such as pause, play, and so on.

`autobuffer` lets the browser handle the buffering and streaming. The `autobuffer` attribute has Boolean value. If it is in audio tag; audio will buffer automatically. `preload=auto` makes the stream preload even before playing.

A problem with audio streaming on mobile is the format support. Here is a table showing the support comparison:

Browser	Ogg Vorbis	MP3	WAV
Android WebKit	Yes	Yes	
Opera Mobile		Yes	
Firefox Mobile	Yes		Yes
iOS Safari		Yes	Yes

As shown in the table, the support has been largely inconsistent. This can be quite troublesome for cross-browser audio streaming. One way you can do it is to use multiple tracks. If a browser can't recognize a track in the first source tags, it will just try the next one. As we can see from the preceding table, the most widely supported format is MP3.

It is supported by most mobile browsers except Firefox. For Firefox, we can use Ogg, so the following code is more cross-mobile browser compatible:

```
<!doctype html>
<html>
  <head>
    <title>Mobile Cookbook</title>
    <meta charset="utf-8">
    <meta name="viewport" content="width=device-width,
initial-scale=1.0">
  </head>
  <body>

    <div id="main">
      <audio controls preload="auto" autobuffer>
        <source src="resources/snake_charmer.mp3" />
        <source src="resources/snake_charmer.ogg" />
      </audio>
    </div>

  </body>
</html>
```

There's more...

You may ask, 'What about browsers that don't support HTML5 audio tags?' There are audio polyfills, but generally, I don't see the point of using polyfills for mobile audio. One reason is because these polyfills are made using Flash, and Flash Lite is only supported on limited mobile devices such as Symbian. One solution is to simply include a link within the audio tags. It won't be rendered by browsers that support audio tags, but it will show on browsers that don't support audio tags. You can do so by adding a download link inside just before the closing audio tags:

```
<div id="main">
  <audio controls preload="auto" autobuffer>
            <a href="resources/snake_charmer.mp3">play or
download here</a>
  </audio>
</div>
```

Now if you render this in Windows Phone, the following will be displayed:

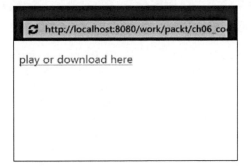

And if you click on the link, it will simply be opened by the system's default music player:

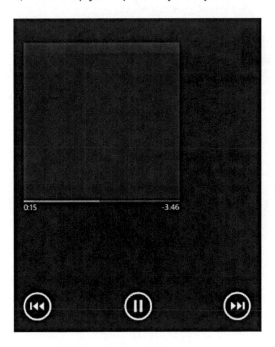

W3C Audio Working Group

The current audio element lacks a client-side API. W3C Audio Working Group (http://www.w3.org/2011/audio/) was set up to address this issue. The API will support the features required by advanced interactive applications including the ability to process and synthesize audio streams directly in script. You can subscribe to participate in the discussion at: public-audio-request@w3.org.

Streaming video on your mobile

Target browsers: iOS, Android, Blackberry, webOS, Opera Mobile, Firefox Mobile

Some of the most visited websites from desktop platforms are video sites such as `http://www.youtube.com` and `http://www.vimeo.com`. They have a version optimized for mobiles. Video streaming is an important part of mobile. People enjoy watching videos on the go, especially short videos such as those on YouTube. They take less time to buffer and it doesn't take much time to finish watching. So how does the video work on a mobile device? Let's first create an example.

Getting ready

Create an HTML document named `ch06r02.html`.

How to do it...

Enter the following code in to the HTML document:

```
<!doctype html>
<html>
  <head>
    <title>Mobile Cookbook</title>
    <meta charset="utf-8">
    <meta name="viewport" content="width=device-width, initial-scale=1.0">
  </head>
  <body>

    <div id="main">
      <video id="movie" width="320" height="240" preload controls>
        <source src=" http://diveintohtml5.info/i/test.mp4" />
        <source src=" http://diveintohtml5.info/i/pr6.webm"
type='video/webm; codecs="vp8, vorbis"' />
        <source src=" http://diveintohtml5.info/i/pr6.ogv"
type='video/ogg; codecs="theora, vorbis"' />
        <object width="320" height="240" type="application/x-
shockwave-flash"data=" http://releases.flowplayer.org/swf/flowplayer-
3.2.1.swfflowplayer-3.2.1.swf"> data="flowplayer-3.2.1.swf">
          <param name="movie" value=" http://releases.flowplayer.org/
swf/flowplayer-3.2.1.swf" />
          <param name="allowfullscreen" value="true" />
          <param name="flashvars" value='config={"clip":
{"url":http://diveintohtml5.info/i//test.mp4", "autoPlay":false,
"autoBuffering":true}}' />
```

```
        <p>Download video as <a href=" http://diveintohtml5.
info/i/pr6.mp4">MP4</a>, <a href=" http://diveintohtml5.info/i/
pr6.webm">WebM</a>, or <a href=" http://diveintohtml5.info/i/pr6.
ogv">Ogg</a>.</p>
        </object>
      </video>
      <p>Try this page in Safari 4! Or you can <a href=" http://
diveintohtml5.info/i//test.mp4">download the video</a> instead.</p>
    </div>

  </body>
</html>
```

Now if you open it in a mobile browser, you should see the video player rendered.

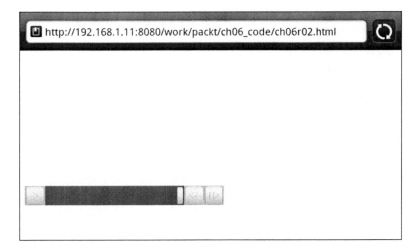

How it works...

Part of the code is taken from *Mark Pilgrim's Dive into HTML5*. You must be thinking, that's a hell of a lot of work to get video working! Here let's see what each part does. Both iOS and Android support H.264 (mp4) format, webm and ogv versions are added to make sure it will also render in other desktop and mobile devices.

If you have multiple <source> elements, iOS will only recognize the first one. Since iOS devices only support H.264+AAC+MP4, you have to always list your MP4 first. This bug is fixed in iOS 4.0. So in the example, we listed test.mp4 as the first one.

```
<source src=" http://diveintohtml5.info/i/test.mp4" />
<source src=" http://diveintohtml5.info/i/pr6.webm" type='video/webm;
codecs="vp8, vorbis"' />
<source src=" http://diveintohtml5.info/i/pr6.ogv" type='video/ogg;
codecs="theora, vorbis"' />
```

The following Flash fallback is added to make sure sites don't support HTML5 video could play the video:

```
<object width="320" height="240" type="application/x-shockwave-
flash"data=" http://releases.flowplayer.org/swf/flowplayer-
3.2.1.swfflowplayer-3.2.1.swf"> data="flowplayer-3.2.1.swf">
<param name="movie" value=" http://releases.flowplayer.org/swf/
flowplayer-3.2.1.swf" />
<param name="allowfullscreen" value="true" />
<param name="flashvars" value='config={"clip": {"url": "resources
http://diveintohtml5.info/i//test.mp4", "autoPlay":false,
"autoBuffering":true}}' />
<p>Download video as <a href="test.mp4">MP4</a>, <a href="test.
webm">WebM</a>, or <a href="test.ogv">Ogg</a>.</p>
</object>
```

There's more...

Mark Pilgrim's Dive into HTML5 has detailed information about issues that are faced while rendering a video on different browsers. You can have a read at: `http://diveintohtml5.info/video.html`

Versions of Android before 2.3 had a couple of issues with HTML5 video. The type attribute on `<source>` elements confused earlier versions of Android greatly. The only way to get it to recognize a video source is, ironically, to omit the type attribute altogether and ensure that your H.264+AAC+MP4 video file's name ends with a `.mp4` extension. You can still include the type attribute on your other video sources, as H.264 is the only video format that Android 2.2 supports. This bug is fixed in Android 2.3.

The `controls` attribute was not supported. There are no ill effects to including it, but Android will not display any user interface controls for a video. You will need to provide your own user interface controls. As a minimum, you should provide a script that starts playing the video when the user clicks it. This bug is also fixed in Android 2.3.

Using offline caching

Target browsers: iOS, Android, Opera Mobile, webOS, Firefox Mobile

Apart from Device Access, offline caching is one of the most important features for mobile devices. One of the biggest differences between desktop browsing and mobile browsing is that mobile users are always on the go. Unlike desktop browsing, which typically uses a single stable connection, mobile browsing may take place in transit, switching between 3G and WiFi and going offline entirely in such places as tunnels. Offline caching can help with issues caused by disconnection from the Internet.

Devices	Supported
iOS	Yes (3.2+)
Android	Yes (2.1+)
Windows Mobile	No
Blackberry v6.0 and above	No
Symbian 60	No
Palm webOS	Yes
Opera Mobile	Yes
Firefox Mobile	Yes

Getting ready

Let's create a text file and name it `default.appcache`.

How to do it...

In the `default.appcache` file we've just created, type in the following content:

```
CACHE MANIFEST
# version 1
img/apple-touch-icon.png
#img/splash.png
NETWORK:
#http://example.com/api/

FALLBACK:
```

Now create an HTML document and name it ch06r03.html:

```
<!doctype html>
<html manifest="default.appcache">
<head>
<title>Mobile Cookbook</title>
<meta charset="utf-8">
<meta name="viewport" content="width=device-width, initial-scale=1.0">
</head>
<body>
  <img src="img/apple-touch-icon.png" alt="Apple Touch Icon" />
</body>
</html>
```

Now if you load the page, disable the Internet connection and load the page again. You can see the page still loads.

How it works...

Anything under the CACHE MANIFEST comprises the files that will be cached for offline viewing. The file that includes the cache manifest file will automatically be included and that means:

```
CACHE MANIFEST
# version 1
img/apple-touch-icon.png
#img/splash.png
```

The NETWORK section lists all the URLs you DON'T want to be cached. These are the files that should be loaded each time the page is reloaded. An example of such a file is API calls. You don't want the browser to cache dynamic API returns. If all your API calls are from the same prefix, you don't have to include them all. Instead, you only have to include the **prefix**. For example, if you have a list of URLs as follows:

```
http://example.com/api/?loc=paris
http://example.com/api/?loc=london
```

Instead of adding them one by one to the list, you can just add one:

```
NETWORK:
http://example.com/api/
```

The FALLBACK section is a place to list page URL replacements for network URLs to be used when the browser is offline or the remote server is not available.

There's more...

One question you might be asking is why do we use `.appcache` instead of `.manifest` as the extension? It is because `.appcache` is recommended by WHATWG. As it is a standard and there is no issue with browser support, it is best to use `.appcache`.

Another thing you might be wondering is whether these extensions are recognized by the browsers. No worries, the following `AddType` will help both `.appcache` and `.manifest` render with the proper MIME type. Add the following to the `.htaccess` file:

```
AddType text/cache-manifest appcache manifest
```

Appcache facts

To know more about Appcache, one can go over to the *Appcache Facts* site (`http://appcachefacts.info/`). It has much useful and valuable information about Appcache. It also maintains a list of links to sites exploring Appcache:

- Dive Into HTML5 – Let's Take This Offline: (`http://diveintohtml5.info/offline.html`)
- Google Code blog – Using AppCache to Launch Offline: (`http://googlecode.blogspot.com/2009/04/gmail-for-mobile-html5-series-using.html`)
- HTML5 Rocks – A Beginner's Guide to Using the Application Cache: (`http://www.html5rocks.com/tutorials/appcache/beginner/`)
- MDN Doc Center – Offline resources in Firefox: (`https://developer.mozilla.org/en/offline_resources_in_firefox`)
- Safari Developer Library – Storing Data on the Client: (`http://developer.apple.com/library/safari/#documentation/appleapplications/reference/SafariWebContent/Client-SideStorage/Client-SideStorage.html`)
- Cache Manifest Validator – Online validator, JSON(P) validation API, and `TextMate` bundle: (`http://manifest-validator.com/`)

WHATWG's official description

If you want to dig deeper into specs, read the official description of the HTML Living Standard at:

`http://www.whatwg.org/specs/web-apps/current-work/multipage/offline.html`

Using Web Storage on mobile

Target browsers: cross-browser

Web Storage is very useful for offline applications, especially news feeds or e-mail web apps. When people talk about Web Storage, they usually mean the `localStorage` part. It is a key/value persistence system. Apart from web storage, there are two more HTML5 storage features; they are **Indexed Database API** and **Web SQL Database**.

So let's see the pros and cons of Web Storage, Indexed Database, and Web SQL Database.

Storage type	Pros	Cons
Web Storage	Simple, easy to use API	No data privacy
	Supported by major browsers	
Indexed Database	No SQL-like structured storage	Not yet supported by most mobile browsers
		No SQL (obviously)
Web SQL Database	Fast	W3C working group has put in on hold on the standard
	Feature-rich SQL implementation	
	Supported by major new mobile browsers	

From a mobile browser support perspective, Web Storage is the most widely supported, followed by Web SQL Database.

Web SQL Database has a better feature set than Web Storage. So in this recipe, we will focus on Web Storage and Web SQL Database, and not on Indexed Database (at least for now).

Getting ready

Create an HTML document and name it `ch06r04.html`.

How to do it...

First, enter the following code:

```
<!doctype html>
<html>
<head>
<title>Mobile Cookbook</title>
<meta charset="utf-8">
<meta name="viewport" content="width=device-width, initial-scale=1.0">
<script src="js/modernizr.custom.54685.js"></script>
</head>
<body>
  <section>
    <p>Values are stored on <code>keyup</code></p>
    <p>Content loaded from previous sessions:</p>
    <div id="previous"></div>
  </section>
  <section>
    <div>
      <label for="local">localStorage:</label>
      <input type="text" name="local" value="" id="local" />
    </div>
```

Now we are adding in the JavaScript portion:

```
    <script>

var addEvent = (function () {
    if (document.addEventListener) {
      return function (el, type, fn) {
        if (el && el.nodeName || el === window) {
          el.addEventListener(type, fn, false);
        } else if (el && el.length) {
          for (var i = 0; i < el.length; i++) {
            addEvent(el[i], type, fn);
          }
        }
      };
    } else {
      return function (el, type, fn) {
        if (el && el.nodeName || el === window) {
          el.attachEvent('on' + type, function () { return
fn.call(el, window.event); });
```

```
            } else if (el && el.length) {
              for (var i = 0; i < el.length; i++) {
                addEvent(el[i], type, fn);
              }
            }
          };
        }
      })();
    function getStorage(type) {
      var storage = window[type + 'Storage'],
        delta = 0,
        li = document.createElement('li');

      if (!window[type + 'Storage']) return;

      if (storage.getItem('value')) {
        delta = ((new Date()).getTime() - (new Date()).
setTime(storage.getItem('timestamp'))) / 1000;

        li.innerHTML = type + 'Storage: ' + storage.getItem('value') +
' (last updated: ' + delta + 's ago)';
      } else {
        li.innerHTML = type + 'Storage is empty';
      }

      document.querySelector('#previous').appendChild(li);
    }

    getStorage('local');

    addEvent(document.querySelector('#local'), 'keyup', function () {
      localStorage.setItem('value', this.value);
      localStorage.setItem('timestamp', (new Date()).getTime());
    });

    </script>
```

Now at the end of the file, let's close the HTML document:

```
    </section>
  </body>
  </html>
```

`localStorage` even works in Dolphin, a browser used by Samsung and that can be installed on any Android device. When rendering the page using the Dolphin browser, you can enter any words. For this case, if you enter "hullo world", once you hit refresh, it will display this information:

How it works...

As mentioned, it is really as simple as value/key pair, and you can store data using `set` and `get` methods.

To set data, you use `setItem` method:

```
localStorage.setItem('value', this.value);
```

To get data, you use:

```
storage.getItem('value')
```

Looking for a polyfill? jQuery Offline is a nice offline storage plugin. It uses the HTML5 `localStorage` API for persistence. You can use the same API for browsers that do not support `localStorage`. jQuery Offline will simply fall back to making a request to the server each time. You can learn more about it at `https://github.com/wycats/jquery-offline`.

There's more...

Web SQL Database is an alternative to `localStorage`, and it's loved by people who use SQL. *Remy Sharp* has a very good demo on github that shows how to use Web SQL Database. You can learn more about it at: `http://html5demos.com/database`.

Web Storage portability layer

The Web Storage Portability Layer library allows you to write offline storage code easily for browsers that support either HTML5 databases or Gears.

Gears is an earlier offline storage system developed by Google. It is supported on browsers like IE6 and IE Mobile 4.0.1, but it is no longer under development.

You can learn more about this library at: `http://google-opensource.blogspot.com/2009/05/web-storage-portability-layer-common.html`.

HTML5 storage wars

You can read more about localStorage vs. IndexedDB vs. Web SQL at: `http://csimms.botonomy.com/2011/05/html5-storage-wars-localstorage-vs-indexeddb-vs-web-sql.html`.

Using web workers

Target browsers: Opera Mobile, Firefox Mobile, iOS5, Blackberry

Most programmers with Java/Python/.NET backgrounds should be familiar with multi-threaded or concurrent programming. JavaScript was once laughed at for its lack of high-level threading, but with the advent of HTML5 its API has been expanded to allow concurrency, substantially increasing its effective power! JavaScript is no longer just a scripting language. With more and more sophisticated tasks created using JavaScript, it has to perform more while dealing with heavy frontend computing.

Devices	Supported
iOS	Yes (5.0+)
Android	No
Windows Mobile	No
Blackberry	Yes (6.0+)
Symbian	No
Palm webOS	No
Opera Mobile	Yes
Firefox Mobile	Yes

Getting ready

Let's create a JavaScript file and name it `math.js`.

How to do it...

Enter the following code into the document:

```
/* math.js */

function addNumbers(x,y) {
   return x + y;
}

function minNumbers(x,y) {
```

```
    return x - y;
  }

  /*
    Add an eventlistener to the worker, this will
    be called when the worker receives a message
    from the main page.
  */
  this.onmessage = function (event) {
    var data = event.data;

    switch(data.op) {
    case 'mult':
      postMessage(minNumbers(data.x, data.y));
      break;
    case 'add':
      postMessage(addNumbers(data.x, data.y));
      break;
    default:
      postMessage("Wrong operation specified");
    }
  };
```

Now, let's create an HTML document and name it `ch06r05.html`. Enter the following code into the HTML file:

```
<!doctype html>
<html>
<head>
<title>Mobile Cookbook</title>
<meta charset="utf-8">
<meta name="viewport" content="width=device-width, initial-scale=1.0">
<script src="js/modernizr.custom.54685.js"></script>
</head>
<body onload="loadDeals()">
  <input type="text" id="x" value="6" />
  <br />
  <input type="text" id="y" value="3" />
  <br />
  <input type="text" id="output" />
  <br />
  <input type="button" id="minusButton" value="Subtract" />
  <input type="button" id="addButton" value="Add" />
  <script>
  if (Modernizr.webworkers){
```

```
      alert('hi');
   }


   /* Create a new worker */
   arithmeticWorker = new Worker("js/math.js");
   /*
     Add an event listener to the worker, this will
     be called whenever the worker posts any message.
   */
   arithmeticWorker.onmessage = function (event) {
     document.getElementById("output").value = event.data;
   };
   /* Register events for buttons */
   document.getElementById("minusButton").onclick = function() {
     /* Get the values to do operation on */
     x = parseFloat(document.getElementById("x").value);
     y = parseFloat(document.getElementById("y").value);
     message = {
       'op'  : 'min',
       'x'   : x,
       'y'   : y
     };
     arithmeticWorker.postMessage(message);
   }
   document.getElementById("addButton").onclick = function() {
     /* Get the values to do operation on */
     x = parseFloat(document.getElementById("x").value);
     y = parseFloat(document.getElementById("y").value);
     message = {
       'op'  : 'add',
       'x'   : x,
       'y'   : y
     };

     arithmeticWorker.postMessage(message);
   }
   </script>
</body>
</html>
```

While rendering this page in a mobile browser, we can see three fields and two buttons for calculation. In the following example screenshot, I entered 6 and 3 and pressed the **Add** button to see 9 shown as the result:

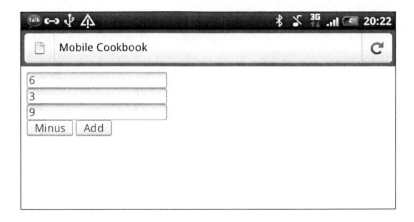

How it works...

We can break math.js into three parts:

- ▸ The actual math functions
- ▸ get event from master (HTML document)
- ▸ post event to master (HTML document)

The actual math functions are fairly easy to understand, addNumbers is a function to add numbers and minNumbers is for deduction:

```
/* math.js */

function addNumbers(x,y) {
   return x + y;
}

function minNumbers(x,y) {
   return x - y;
}
```

The next is the onmessage. This is the information the math.js gets from the HTML document:

```
this.onmessage = function (event) {
   var data = event.data;

   ...
};
```

Once the `math.js` worker gets the information from the master (HTML document), it will start to do the math and post back to the master by using `postMessage`:

```
switch(data.op) {
  case 'mult':
    postMessage(minNumbers(data.x, data.y));
    break;
  case 'add':
    postMessage(addNumbers(data.x, data.y));
    break;
  default:
    postMessage("Wrong operation specified");
}
```

In the HTML document also, there are three parts as follows:

- Create a worker
- `post` information to worker to do the math
- `get` the math done by worker

It is fairly easy to create a worker. It's created by calling `new Worker("math.js")`:

```
/* Create a new worker */
arithmeticWorker = new Worker("js/math.js");
```

For posting information to the worker, you can use the same `postMessage` method as explained in `math.js`. The message itself can be an object with name/value pairs:

```
message = {
  'op' : 'min',
  'x'  : x,
  'y'  : y
};
arithmeticWorker.postMessage(message);
```

For getting the information back once the math is done by the worker, we use the same `onmessage` method explained in `math.js`:

```
arithmeticWorker.onmessage = function (event) {
    document.getElementById("output").value = event.data;
};
```

Creating Flash-like navigation with session and history API

Target browsers: cross-browser

In the past, people had to use hash-tag to fake URL as a compromise between SEO and smooth page transition. Now, with the history API, that hack is no longer needed. With the history API together with Ajax calls, one can dynamically update a URL.

Device platform	Supported
iOS	Yes (4.2+)
Android	Yes (2.2+)
Windows Mobile	No
Blackberry	No
Symbian	Yes (5.2+)
Palm webOS	No
Opera Mobile	No
Firefox Mobile	Yes

Getting ready

Let's create an HTML document and name it `ch06r06.html`.

How to do it...

Enter the following code in the HTML document:

```
<!doctype html>
<html>
<head>
<title>Mobile Cookbook</title>
<meta charset="utf-8">
<meta name="viewport" content="width=device-width, initial-scale=1.0">
<script src="js/modernizr.custom.54685.js"></script>
<style>
section {width:300px; background:#ccc; padding:5px; margin:20px auto;}
html, body, figure {padding:0; margin:0;}
```

```
figcaption {display:block;}
</style>
</head>
<body>
  <section id="gallery">
    <p class="photonav"><a id="photoprev" href="ch06r06_b.html">&lt;
Previous</a> <a id="photonext" href="ch06r06_a.html">Next ></a></p>
    <figure id="photo">
      <img id="photoimg" src="http://placekitten.com/300/300"
alt="Fer" width="300" height="300"><br />
      <figcaption>Adagio, 1982</figcaption>
    </figure>
  </section>
  <script src="js/nav.js"></script>
</body>
</html>
```

Now let's create another document and name it `ch06r06_a.html`. Enter the following code into it:

```
<p class="photonav"><a id="photoprev" href="ch06r06_b.html">&lt;
Previous</a> <a id="photonext" href="ch06r06_b.html">Next ></a></p>
<figure id="photo">
  <img id="photoimg" src="http://placekitten.com/300/301" alt="Fer"
width="300" height="300">
  <figcaption>Aida, 1990</figcaption>
</figure>
```

Now let's create yet another document and name it `ch06r06_b.html`. Enter the following code to the document:

```
<p class="photonav"><a id="photoprev" href="ch06r06_a.html">&lt;
Previous</a> <a id="photonext" href="ch06r06_a.html">Next ></a></p>
<figure id="photo">
  <img id="photoimg" src="http://placekitten.com/300/299" alt="Fer"
width="300" height="300">
  <figcaption>Air Cat, 2001</figcaption>
</figure>
```

Now let's create a JavaScript file and enter the following code. Replace the URL in the following code with your own URL:

```
function supports_history_api() {
  return !!(window.history && history.pushState);
}
```

```
function swapPhoto(href) {
  var req = new XMLHttpRequest();
  req.open("GET",
  "http://localhost /work/packt/ch06_code/" +
  href.split("/").pop(),
  false);
  req.send(null);
  if (req.status == 200) {
    document.getElementById("gallery").innerHTML = req.responseText;
    setupHistoryClicks();
    return true;
  }
  return false;
}

function addClicker(link) {
  link.addEventListener("click", function(e) {
    if (swapPhoto(link.href)) {
      history.pushState(null, null, link.href);
      e.preventDefault();
    }
  }, true);
}

function setupHistoryClicks() {
  addClicker(document.getElementById("photonext"));
  addClicker(document.getElementById("photoprev"));
}

window.onload = function() {
  if (!supports_history_api()) { return; }
  setupHistoryClicks();
  window.setTimeout(function() {
    window.addEventListener("popstate", function(e) {
      swapPhoto(location.pathname);
    }, false);
  }, 1);
}
```

Now let's render the page in a mobile browser. When you click on the **Previous** or **Next** buttons, the pages will not refresh. But if you take a look at the URLs, they are updated:

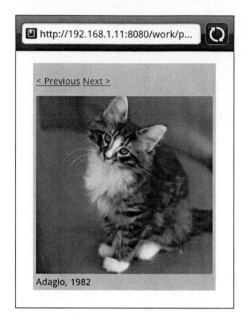

How it works...

`history.pushState` is used to push the new URL to the browser address bar:

```
history.pushState(null, null, link.href);
```

The actual page navigation is an Ajax request to the server, so the page never reloads. But the URL is updated with the following function:

```
function swapPhoto(href) {
  var req = new XMLHttpRequest();
  req.open("GET",
  "http://192.168.1.11:8080/work/packt/ch06_code/" +
  href.split("/").pop(),
  false);
  req.send(null);
  if (req.status == 200) {
    document.getElementById("gallery").innerHTML = req.responseText;
    setupHistoryClicks();
    return true;
  }
  return false;
}
```

There's more...

To learn more about history API, you can dig into the specification at: `http://www.whatwg.org/specs/web-apps/current-work/multipage/history.html`

Mark Pilgrim has a great detailed explanation at *Dive into HTML5*: `http://diveintohtml5.info/history.html`

You can also learn more at *Mozilla's MDC Docs*: `https://developer.mozilla.org/en/DOM/Manipulating_the_browser_history`

Place Kitten

Wondering where the kitten pictures have come from? It's from a site called `http://placekitten.com/`. A quick and simple service for getting pictures of kittens for using them as placeholders in your designs or code.

7
Mobile Debugging

In this chapter, we will cover:

- ▸ Remote debugging with Opera Dragonfly
- ▸ Remote debugging with weinre
- ▸ Using Firebug on mobile
- ▸ Remote debugging with JS Console
- ▸ Setting up Mobile Safari debugging

Introduction

Although debugging can take a significant amount of time, it is an important aspect of web development, both for desktop and mobile. In this chapter, we will go through some of the mobile debugging tools used to make frontend debugging easier, faster, and make web development more productive.

Remote debugging with Opera Dragonfly

Target browser: Opera Mobile

Mobile debugging is different from desktop debugging due to the relatively smaller mobile screen.

Getting ready

1. Make sure you are on a WiFi network.
2. Download the latest version of Opera desktop browser at http://www.opera.com/.
3. Download Opera Mobile on your mobile device.

How to do it...

1. At the time of writing, Opera is at version 11.50. Some of these instructions may change by the time you read the book.

2. Open up Opera on your desktop, and from the drop-down menu, choose **Page | Developer Tools | Opera Dragonfly**.

3. You should see a debugger tool appear at the bottom of the page. Click on **Remote debug configuration**, as shown in the following screenshot:

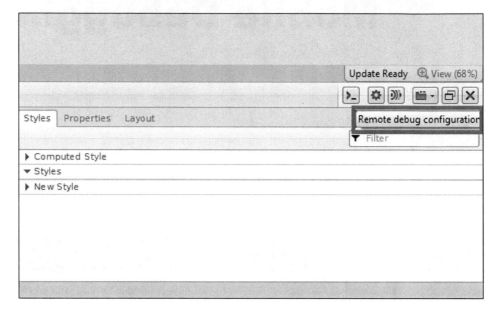

4. Once we click on the **Remote debug configuration** button, there will be a pop-up panel.

5. On the panel, you can see a text field to specify a port number and an **Apply** button. The default number should be unused and should work fine. Click on **Apply**:

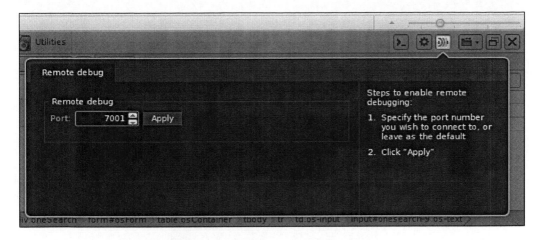

6. Now fire up your desktop console and type in `ipconfig` as the command. The IPv4 address is your IP address.

7. Open Opera Mobile on a mobile device, type `opera:debug` in the URL address bar, and we will arrive at a page as follows:

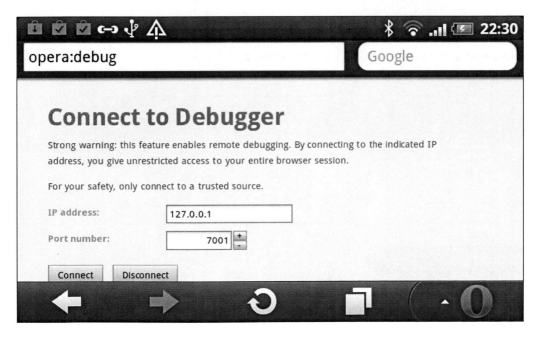

8. Enter the IP address you got from the desktop console, and click on **Connect**. Now the mobile browser should be connected to Dragonfly:

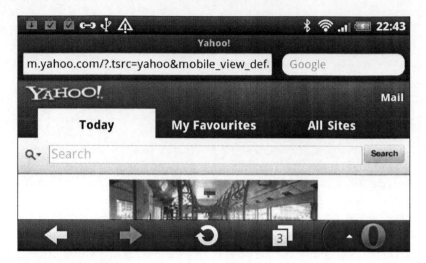

How it works...

Open a new tab on Opera Mobile, visit Yahoo.com, now switch to desktop, and click on **Select the debugging context**, which is the fourth button at the upper-right corner. Select **Yahoo!** from the drop-down to start inspecting the page!

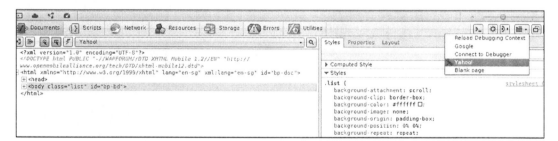

See also

▶ *Remote debugging with weinre*

▶ *Remote debugging with JS Console*

Remote debugging with weinre

Target browsers: iOS, Android, Blackberry, webOS

In the previous recipe, we saw how you can debug Opera mobile pages remotely. In this recipe, we will see how we can debug remotely in other mobile devices. **Weinre** is a **Web Inspector Remote**.

The supported OS include:

- Android 2.2 Browser application
- Android 2.2 w/PhoneGap 0.9.2iOS 4.2.x
- Mobile Safari application
- BlackBerry v6.x simulator
- webOS 2.x (unspecified version)

Getting ready

First, we must download weinre from the official website; there are two versions available, one for PC and one for Mac:

```
https://github.com/phonegap/weinre/archives/master
```

How to do it...

1. First, get your IP address by running `ipconfig` in your console.
2. Create an HTML document and name it `ch07r01.html`. Replace `192.168.1.11` with your own IP address:

```
<!doctype html>
<html>
  <head>
    <title>Mobile Cookbook</title>
    <meta charset="utf-8">
    <meta name="viewport" content="width=device-width, initial-
scale=1.0">

  </head>
  <body>
    <header>
      <h1>Mobile Cookbook</h1>
    </header>
```

```
      <div id="main">
      </div>

      <script src="http://192.168.1.11:8081/target/target-script-
min.js"></script>
    </body>
</html>
```

3. First, locate the downloaded `weinre.jar` file. In my case, the path is `C:\xampp\htdocs\dev\weinre.jar`. Second, get the IP address, in my case, `http://192.168.1.11`.

4. Now fire up your console and type the following line:

   `java -jar path/to/weinre.jar -httpPort 8081 -boundHost http://192.168.1.11`

5. To test if it works, visit the URL address `http://192.168.1.11:8081/`, a page close to the following screenshot should appear:

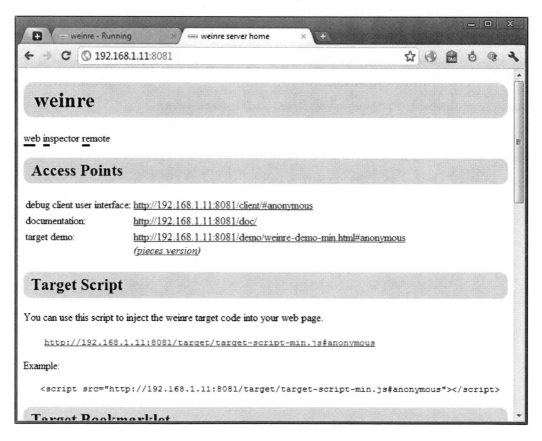

How it works...

Now use your mobile device to access the sample page created:

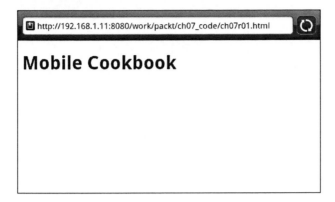

Now, back on the desktop, click on **Debug client user interface**. Do not open a tab, but open in a new window.

You should be able to see something like the following screenshot:

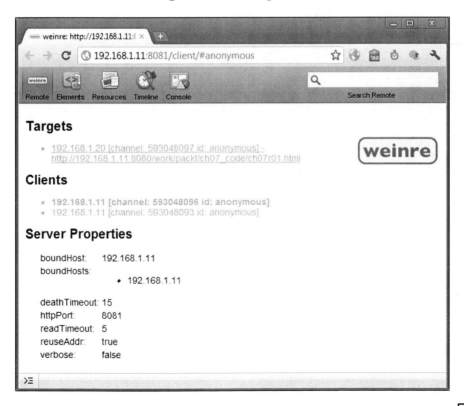

Click on **Elements**, and now you can inspect the elements (as shown in the following screenshot):

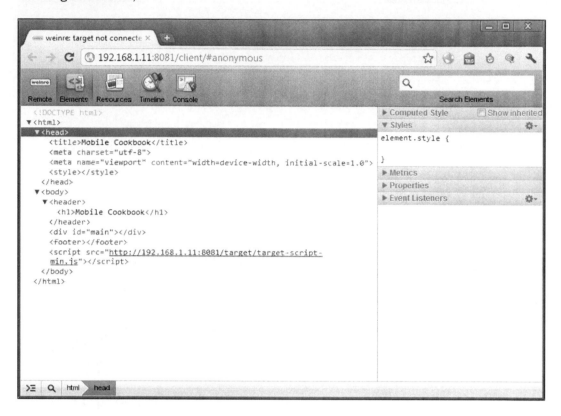

Using Firebug on mobile

Target browsers: cross-browser

Many people use Firebug on Firefox and Chrome, but Firebug Lite can be used on any browser that supports JavaScript. In this recipe, we will see how to use Firebug to debug.

Getting ready

Create an HTML document and name it `ch07r02.html`.

How to do it...

1. Enter the following code in HTML:

```html
<!doctype html>
<html>
  <head>
    <title>Mobile Cookbook</title>
    <meta charset="utf-8">
    <meta name="viewport" content="width=device-width,
initial-scale=1.0">

  </head>
  <body>

    <div id="main">
    </div>

    <script type="text/javascript" src="https://getfirebug.com/
firebug-lite.js"></script>
  </body>
</html>
```

2. Render it in a mobile browser:

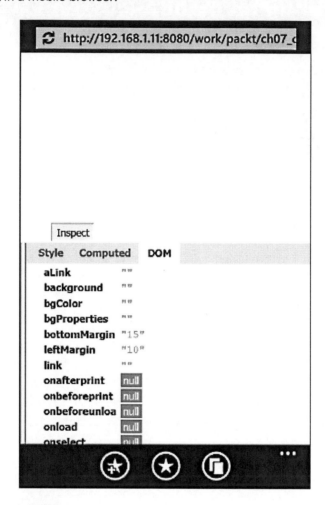

How it works...

Firebug Lite is a JavaScript version of Firebug. The following line of code will load Firebug Lite script hosted on the Firebug site:

```
<script type="text/javascript" src="https://getfirebug.com/firebug-
lite.js"></script>
```

You can also download the script and add it as a local version.

You can access HTML, CSS, and JavaScript, and view the DOM. The console can be used for JavaScript input.

There are four distribution channels for Firebug Lite:

- ▶ **Stable channel**
- ▶ **Debug channel**
- ▶ **Beta channel**
- ▶ **Developer channel**

The one we have been using is the stable channel. Other channels are explained under the *There's more* section.

There's more...

Apart from the live and local version, you can also add the bookmarklet. It may not work on all browsers. Here is how it can be done.

1. Click on the links on the right-hand side of the page: `http://getfirebug.com/ firebuglite`

> **Bookmarklets**
> Firebug Lite
> Firebug Lite debug
> Firebug Lite beta

2. This adds the hash `#javascript:(function...` to the end of the URL in the mobile browser.

3. Bookmark the page on Safari.

4. Edit the bookmark's name to be the name of the bookmarklet, Firebug Lite, Firebug Lite debug or Firebug Lite beta.

5. After you save the bookmark, open the bookmark menu, select **Firebug Lite** and click on **Edit**. Delete the URL and the #, so only the part that starts with `javascript:(function` remains.

6. Now if you open any web page and tap on **Firebug Lite bookmark**, a Firebug console will appear at the bottom-right corner of the page.

Debug channel

The debug channel uses the same version as the stable channel, but with different pre-configurations to make it easier to debug Firebug Lite itself.

Beta channel

The beta channel is where the new features and fixes are polished. It should be considerably stable (no known regression), but it may contain some bugs and some features may be incomplete.

Developer channel

The developer channel is where the ideas get created and tested. Once it is tied directly to our code repository, you'll get the most recent code possible and will receive updates much more frequently than other channels. One thing to be aware of, however, is that the developer channel can be very unstable at times and the initial load can be slower.

Remote JavaScript debugging with JS Console

Target browsers: cross-browser

If you only look for remote JavaScript debugging, *Remy Sharp* has an awesome tool named JavaScript Console. It is really productive for mobile debugging.

Getting ready

Visit `http://jsconsole.com/` and you will see a page as shown next:

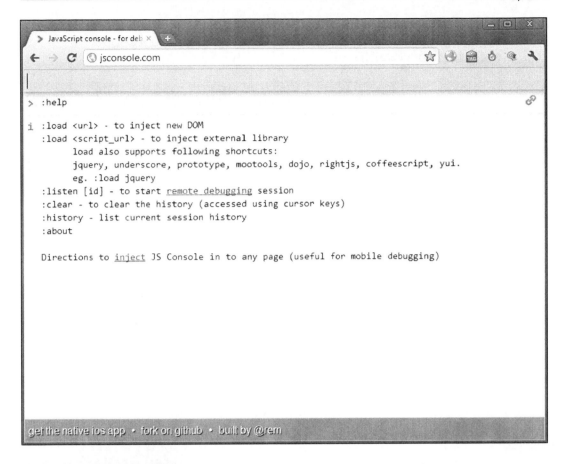

How to do it...

1. Enter :listen on the site, and you should see the following info messages returning:

    Creating connection ...

    Connected to "65C1F9F1-6A57-46C0-96BB-35C5B515331F"

2. This will be followed by a line of JavaScript looking like:

<script src="http://jsconsole.com/remote.js?65C1F9F1-6A57-46C0-96BB-35C5B515331F"></script>

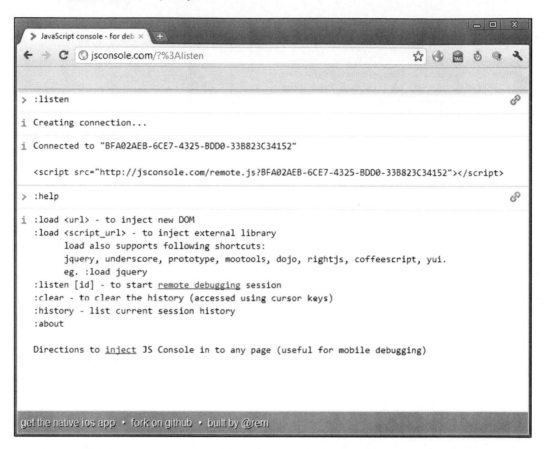

3. Create an HTML page and name it `ch07r04.html`. Enter the following code to the document, replace the `<script>...</script>` with your own script that you got from jsconsole.com:

```
<!doctype html>
<html>
  <head>
    <title>Mobile Cookbook</title>
    <meta charset="utf-8">
    <meta name="viewport" content="width=device-width, initial-
scale=1.0">
  </head>
  <body>
    >
```

```
        <div id="main">
        </div>

        <script src="http://jsconsole.com/remote.js?04926BFB-44AB-
    4979-BAE9-F4A4FA7CE22C"></script>
        <script>
        for (var i=0; i<10; i++) {
          console.log('testing '+i);
        }
        </script>
      </body>
    </html>
```

4. Now if we render the page on a mobile device, we will see the desktop screen web page has log messages appearing:

```
« "testing 4"

> remote console.log                                                      🔗

« "testing 3"

i Connection established with http://192.168.1.11:8080/work/packt/ch07_code/ch07r04.html
  Mozilla/5.0 (Linux; U; Android 2.3.3; en-sg; HTC_DesireHD_A9191 Build/GRI40)
  AppleWebKit/533.1 (KHTML, like Gecko) Version/4.0 Mobile Safari/533.1

> remote console.log                                                      🔗

« "testing 2"

> remote console.log                                                      🔗

« "testing 1"

> remote console.log                                                      🔗

« "testing 0"

> :listen                                                                 🔗

i Creating connection...
```

How it works...

In the following loop, we use `console.log` to output a string of messages:

```
<script>
for (var i=0; i<10; i++) {
  console.log('testing '+i);
}
</script>
```

Any calls to `console.log` from your web app will display the result in the jsconsole session that is listening to your key. Equally, if you run a command in the jsconsole session, the code will be injected in to your web app and the result returned to jsconsole.

There's more...

The entire JavaScript Console web app is open source; if you want to learn more about how it was made, visit: `https://github.com/remy/jsconsole`.

JS Console iOS app

JS Console for iOS, also made by *Remy Sharp*, is a JavaScript console to test and inspect the results of your JavaScript without the need to be online or in a browser.

Simple iOS simulator example

This video made by *Remy Sharp* shows how remote debugging JavaScript is done in iOS using jsconsole.com. It shows how to receive logs and send arbitrary commands:

`http://www.youtube.com/watch?v=Y219Ziuipvc&feature=player_embedded`

Remote debugging JavaScript on any device

In the following video, *Remy Sharp* recorded a walk through of how to use jsconsole.com to remotely debug any browser on any device:

`http://www.youtube.com/watch?v=DSH392Gxaho&feature=player_embedded`

Setting up Mobile Safari debugging

Target browsers: iOS

On iOS mobile Safari, there is a built-in debugger for debugging.

Getting ready

Have an iPhone to hand and navigate to the home screen.

How to do it...

1. Find and open the **Settings** application:

2. Select **Safari**:

3. Scroll down to find the **Developer** option at the bottom:

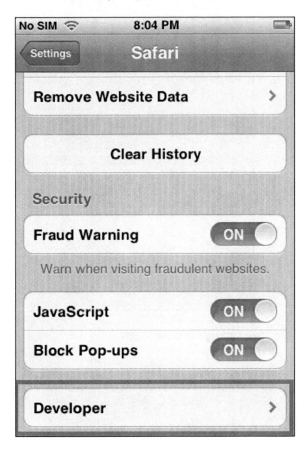

4. By default, the **Debug Console** is **OFF**:

5. Now we can switch the **Debug Console** to **ON**:

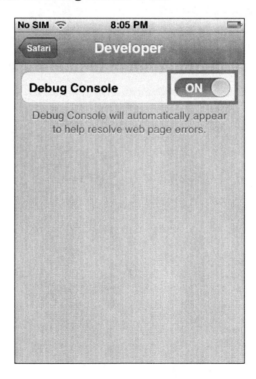

6. In Safari, look for the debug console's summary info at the top of the page, just below the URL bar:

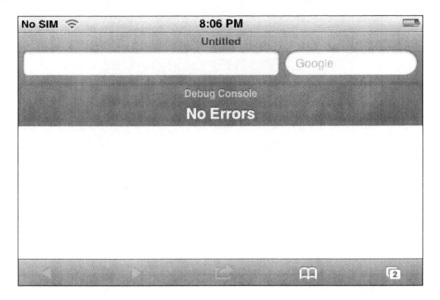

7. Touch the summary info to view a detailed report for the errors on the page.

8. Now, let's create an HTML document and name it ch07r05.html. Enter the following code to the page:

```
<!doctype html>
<html>
    <head>
      <title>Mobile Cookbook</title>
      <meta charset="utf-8">
      <meta name="viewport" content="width=device-width,
initial-scale=1.0">

    </head>
    <body>

      <div id="main">
      </div>

      <script>
      for (var i=0; i<3; i++) {
        console.log('testing '+i);
      }
      </script>
    </body>
</html>
```

9. When rendering it, we can see:

How it works...

Once you click on **Debug Console**, it will bring you to the message screen:

The following script is used to create the debug message:

```
<script>
for (var i=0; i<3; i++) {
  console.log('testing '+i);
}
</script>
```

8
Server-Side Tuning

In this chapter, we will cover:

- ► Preventing mobile transcoding
- ► Adding mobile MIME types
- ► Making cache manifest display properly
- ► Setting far future expire headers
- ► Gzip compression
- ► Entity tag removal

Introduction

Server-side performance directly impacts the page loading speed. Proper server configuration can hugely improve the client-side loading speed.

In this chapter, we will go through some of the server-side configurations used to make mobile websites and applications perform better and faster. Some of the concepts are mobile-centric; some are applicable to the desktop web as well.

There are many server best practice guidelines, but some may not be comprehensive enough. In this chapter, we combine the best of the best practices and see how we can maximize the performance of a site.

Preventing mobile transcoding

Target browsers: cross-browser

Many mobile operators use proxies or adaptation engines to change the content of the web page you want to serve. On many mobile devices, built-in or installed browsers use mobile transcoders to reformat and compress page content. This is called **Mobile Transcoding**. If you don't want the content to be altered, an HTTP header must be added to prevent mobile transcoding.

Getting ready

An .htaccess file is used to configure an Apache server at the file directory level. The configuration can also be done by editing httpd.conf. Because many server hosting companies won't allow access to the root where the Apache is installed, in this example, we use .htaccess. This makes the server configuration at a directory level easier because unlike main httpd.conf, it doesn't require the server to be restarted. Create or open an .htaccess file.

How to do it...

Add the following code to the .htaccess file:

```
<FilesMatch "\.(php|cgi|pl)$">
Header append Cache-Control "no-transform"
Header append Vary "User-Agent, Accept"
</FilesMatch>
```

Upload the .htaccess file to the folder to which you want the rules to apply.

By doing this, we have prevented mobile transcoding from happening.

How it works...

FilesMatch is used to filter only CGI and PHP scripts, because we don't want to apply this rule to other file types.

```
<FilesMatch "\.(php|cgi|pl)$">
```

Provided that Apache module mod_headers is enabled, we can add the header Cache-Control "no-transform" in a FilesMatch section.

```
Header append Cache-Control "no-transform"
```

There's more...

The following resources might be helpful in knowing more about mobile transcoding.

Microsoft Internet Information Server (IIS)

If you are using **Microsoft Internet Information Server** (**IIS**), it can be configured using the software interface. Details about how to do this can be found at:

```
http://mobiforge.com/developing/story/setting-http-headers-advise-
transcoding-proxies
```

Responsible reformatting

The following article provides some insights about the impact of content transcoding done by network operators:

```
http://mobiforge.com/developing/blog/responsible-reformatting
```

MBP – Mobile Boilerplate

The snippet used in this chapter is also included in Mobile Boilerplate:

```
https://github.com/h5bp/mobile-boilerplate/blob/master/.htaccess
```

Adding mobile MIME types

Target browsers: Blackberry, Symbian

There are many mobile-exclusive content types supported by BlackBerry and Nokia browsers. In this topic, we will look at some of the MIME types used by these mobile browsers. As the server might not recognize them by default, it is important to add them correctly in the server configuration.

Getting ready

An .htaccess file is used to configure the Apache server at the file directory level. It makes the server configuration at directory level easy. Create or open an .htaccess file.

How to do it...

Add the following code to the `.htaccess` file:

```
AddType application/x-bb-appworld bbaw
AddType text/vnd.rim.location.xloc xloc
AddType text/x-vcard                 vcf
AddType application/octet-stream sisx
AddType application/vnd.symbian.install sis
```

Upload the `.htaccess` file to the folder at which you want the rules to apply.

How it works...

We make the mobile MIME types recognizable by using `AddType`:

Code	Description
`AddType application/x-bb-appworld bbaw`	A text file that contains the application ID for an application found in the BlackBerry App World™ storefront.
`AddType text/vnd.rim.location.xloc xloc`	A BlackBerry Maps location document.
`AddType text/x-vcard vcf`	A vCard file, a standard file format for electronic business cards.
`AddType application/octet-stream sisx`	Nokia types
`AddType application/vnd.symbian.install sis`	Nokia types

There's more...

For more mobile file types supported by BlackBerry, go to:

```
http://docs.blackberry.com/en/developers/deliverables/18169/index.jsp
?name=Feature+and+Technical+Overview+-+BlackBerry+Browser6.0&language
=English&userType=21&category=BlackBerry+Browser&subCategory=
```

Making cache manifest display properly

Target browsers: cross-browser

As explained in *Chapter 6, Mobile Rich Media*, cache manifest is used for offline web applications. The extensions for this file may not be recognized by the server. Let's see how we can add the proper MIME type.

Getting ready

Create or open an .htaccess file.

How to do it...

Add the following code:

```
AddType text/cache-manifest appcache manifest
```

Upload the .htaccess file to the folder you want the rules to apply.

How it works...

Cache manifest may have either .appcache or .manifest as its extension. By adding both types as text/cache-manifest, we are making sure they can both be rendered correctly regardless of which one is used.

MBP – Mobile Boilerplate

The .htaccess rule is included in the Mobile Boilerplate:

```
https://github.com/h5bp/mobile-boilerplate/blob/master/.htaccess#L75
```

Setting far future expire headers

Target browsers: cross-browser

Setting up far future expire headers for files is used to improve site performance by reducing unnecessary HTTP requests. For a rich media site with many resources to load, this can improve the overall performance. There are different file types and, depending on the use of the file, we choose different periods of time for them to expire.

Getting ready

Create or open an .htaccess file.

How to do it...

Add the following code:

```
<IfModule mod_expires.c>
  ExpiresActive on
  ExpiresDefault                              "access plus 1 month"
  ExpiresByType text/cache-manifest           "access plus 0 seconds"
  ExpiresByType text/html                     "access plus 0 seconds"
  ExpiresByType text/xml                      "access plus 0 seconds"
  ExpiresByType application/xml               "access plus 0 seconds"
  ExpiresByType application/json              "access plus 0 seconds"
  ExpiresByType application/rss+xml           "access plus 1 hour"
  ExpiresByType image/x-icon                  "access plus 1 week"
  ExpiresByType image/gif                     "access plus 1 month"
  ExpiresByType image/png                     "access plus 1 month"
  ExpiresByType image/jpg                     "access plus 1 month"
  ExpiresByType image/jpeg                    "access plus 1 month"
  ExpiresByType video/ogg                     "access plus 1 month"
  ExpiresByType audio/ogg                     "access plus 1 month"
  ExpiresByType video/mp4                     "access plus 1 month"
  ExpiresByType video/webm                    "access plus 1 month"
  ExpiresByType text/x-component              "access plus 1 month"
  ExpiresByType font/truetype                 "access plus 1 month"
  ExpiresByType font/opentype                 "access plus 1 month"
  ExpiresByType application/x-font-woff       "access plus 1 month"
  ExpiresByType image/svg+xml                 "access plus 1 month"
  ExpiresByType application/vnd.ms-fontobject "access plus 1 month"
  ExpiresByType text/css                      "access plus 1 year"
  ExpiresByType application/javascript        "access plus 1 year"
  ExpiresByType text/javascript               "access plus 1 year"
  <IfModule mod_headers.c>
    Header append Cache-Control "public"
  </IfModule>
</IfModule>
```

Upload the .htaccess file to the folder to which you want the rules to apply.

How it works...

Here is the breakdown of the code where we will see how it works:

1. Whitelist Expires rules:

   ```
   ExpiresDefault                          "access plus 1 month"
   ```

2. `cache.appcache` needs re-requests in FF 3.6:

   ```
   ExpiresByType text/cache-manifest       "access plus 0 seconds"
   ```

3. Your document HTML shouldn't be cached:

   ```
   ExpiresByType text/html                 "access plus 0 seconds"
   ```

4. Data shouldn't be cached as it always needs to be pulled:

   ```
   ExpiresByType text/xml                  "access plus 0 seconds"
   ExpiresByType application/xml           "access plus 0 seconds"
   ExpiresByType application/json          "access plus 0 seconds"
   ```

5. RSS feed updates less frequently than normal API data:

   ```
   ExpiresByType application/rss+xml       "access plus 1 hour"
   ```

6. Favicon cannot be renamed, so the best approach is to set it to a week from now:

   ```
   ExpiresByType image/x-icon              "access plus 1 week"
   ```

7. For heavy media resources such as images, video, and audio, we can set the date further in the future:

   ```
   ExpiresByType image/gif                 "access plus 1 month"
   ...
   ExpiresByType video/webm                "access plus 1 month"
   ```

8. HTC files, useful if you use HTML5 polyfill - CSS3PIE:

   ```
   ExpiresByType text/x-component          "access plus 1 month"
   ```

9. It's safe to cache Webfonts for a month:

   ```
   ExpiresByType font/truetype             "access plus 1 month"
   ...
   ExpiresByType application/vnd.ms-fontobject "access plus 1 month"
   ```

10. For CSS and JavaScript, we can set the expiration date to be a year ahead:

    ```
    ExpiresByType text/css                  "access plus 1 year"
    ExpiresByType application/javascript    "access plus 1 year"
    ExpiresByType text/javascript           "access plus 1 year"
    ```

There's more...

These are pretty far-future Expires headers. They assume you control versioning with cache busting query parameters such as:

```
<script src="script_034543.js" ></script>
```

Additionally, consider the possibility that outdated proxies may miscache:

```
http://www.stevesouders.com/blog/2008/08/23/revving-filenames-dont-
use-querystring/
```

Add an Expires or a Cache-Control header

In the Yahoo! Developer Network, there is a pretty good explanation about Expires rules:

```
http://developer.yahoo.com/performance/rules.html#expires
```

Rules in MBP – Mobile Boilerplate

These rules are included in Mobile Boilerplate's `.htacess file`:

```
https://github.com/h5bp/mobile-boilerplate/blob/master/.htaccess#L142
```

Compressing files using Gzip

Target browsers: cross-browser

Frontend developers play an important role in making decisions about how to reduce the time it takes to transfer HTTP requests and responses across the network. Gzip compression can be used to reduce response time by reducing the size of the HTTP response.

Gzip drastically reduces the response size, usually by 70 percent. Gzip is widely supported by modern browsers.

Most servers only compress certain file types by default, so it's best to define rules that support a wide range of text files, including HTML, XML, and JSON.

Getting ready

Create or open an `.htaccess` file.

How to do it...

Add the following code in to `.htaccess`:

```
<IfModule mod_deflate.c>
  <IfModule mod_setenvif.c>
    <IfModule mod_headers.c>
      SetEnvIfNoCase ^(Accept-EncodXng|X-cept-
Encoding|X{15}|~{15}|-{15})$ ^((gzip|deflate)\s,?\s(gzip|deflate)?
|X{4,13}|~{4,13}|-{4,13})$ HAVE_Accept-Encoding
      RequestHeader append Accept-Encoding "gzip,deflate" env=HAVE_
Accept-Encoding
    </IfModule>
  </IfModule>

  <IfModule filter_module>
    FilterDeclare   COMPRESS
    FilterProvider  COMPRESS  DEFLATE resp=Content-Type $text/html
    FilterProvider  COMPRESS  DEFLATE resp=Content-Type $text/css
    FilterProvider  COMPRESS  DEFLATE resp=Content-Type $text/
javascript
    FilterProvider  COMPRESS  DEFLATE resp=Content-Type $text/plain
    FilterProvider  COMPRESS  DEFLATE resp=Content-Type $text/xml
    FilterProvider  COMPRESS  DEFLATE resp=Content-Type $text/x-
component
    FilterProvider  COMPRESS  DEFLATE resp=Content-Type $application/
javascript
    FilterProvider  COMPRESS  DEFLATE resp=Content-Type $application/
json
    FilterProvider  COMPRESS  DEFLATE resp=Content-Type $application/
xml
    FilterProvider  COMPRESS  DEFLATE resp=Content-Type $application/
x-javascript
    FilterProvider  COMPRESS  DEFLATE resp=Content-Type $application/
xhtml+xml
    FilterProvider  COMPRESS  DEFLATE resp=Content-Type $application/
rss+xml
    FilterProvider  COMPRESS  DEFLATE resp=Content-Type $application/
atom+xml
    FilterProvider  COMPRESS  DEFLATE resp=Content-Type $application/
vnd.ms-fontobject
    FilterProvider  COMPRESS  DEFLATE resp=Content-Type $image/svg+xml
```

```
    FilterProvider   COMPRESS   DEFLATE resp=Content-Type $application/
x-font-ttf
    FilterProvider   COMPRESS   DEFLATE resp=Content-Type $font/opentype
    FilterChain      COMPRESS
    FilterProtocol   COMPRESS   DEFLATE change=yes;byteranges=no
  </IfModule>

  <IfModule !mod_filter.c>
    AddOutputFilterByType DEFLATE text/html text/plain text/css
application/json
    AddOutputFilterByType DEFLATE text/javascript application/
javascript application/x-javascript
    AddOutputFilterByType DEFLATE text/xml application/xml text/x-
component
    AddOutputFilterByType DEFLATE application/xhtml+xml application/
rss+xml application/atom+xml
    AddOutputFilterByType DEFLATE image/svg+xml application/vnd.ms-
fontobject application/x-font-ttf font/opentype
  </IfModule>
</IfModule>
```

Upload the `.htaccess` file to the folder to which you want the rules to apply.

How it works...

The following code forces deflation for mangled headers, in order to detect the mangled patterns, `mod_setenvif` is used to perform a regular expression match and set an environment variable indicating the mangled Accept-Encoding header is present:

```
SetEnvIfNoCase ^(Accept-EncodXng|X-cept-Encoding|X{15}|~{15}|-{15})$
^((gzip|deflate)\s,?\s(gzip|deflate)?|X{4,13}|~{4,13}|-{4,13})$ HAVE_
Accept-Encoding
```

Forcing the request header to support compression is straightforward:

```
RequestHeader append Accept-Encoding "gzip,deflate" env=HAVE_Accept-
Encoding
```

Compressing HTML, TXT, CSS, JavaScript, JSON, XML, HTC:

```
<IfModule filter_module>
  FilterDeclare   COMPRESS
  ...
  FilterProtocol   COMPRESS   DEFLATE change=yes;byteranges=no
</IfModule>
```

For legacy versions of Apache prior to version 2.1:

```
<IfModule !mod_filter.c>
    AddOutputFilterByType DEFLATE text/html text/plain text/css
application/json
    AddOutputFilterByType DEFLATE text/javascript application/
javascript application/x-javascript
    AddOutputFilterByType DEFLATE text/xml application/xml text/x-
component
    AddOutputFilterByType DEFLATE application/xhtml+xml application/
rss+xml application/atom+xml
    AddOutputFilterByType DEFLATE image/svg+xml application/vnd.ms-
fontobject application/x-font-ttf font/opentype
</IfModule>
```

There's more...

One thing to note is that images and PDF files need not be gzipped because they are already compressed by default. To gzip them will waste CPU usage and even increase the file sizes.

Pushing Beyond Gzipping

An article about gzipping on Yahoo! Network by *Marcel Duran* talks about the recent research and server-side approach:

```
http://developer.yahoo.com/blogs/ydn/posts/2010/12/pushing-beyond-
gzipping/
```

Removing ETags

Target browsers: cross-browser

ETags stands for **Entity tags**. An entity is a component like a CSS or JavaScript file, an image, and so on. What an entity tag does is to identify a specific version of a component. You can find more details at *Yahoo! Developer Network, High Performance Web Sites: Rule 13 – Configure ETags:* (http://developer.yahoo.com/blogs/ydn/posts/2007/07/high_performanc_11/).

If you have multiple servers hosting your website, for example, on a content delivery network, ETag's validation mechanism may cause extra re-fetching. There is little advantage in the validation model, so the best practice is to just remove the ETag.

Getting ready

Create or open an `.htaccess` file.

How to do it...

Add the following code:

```
<IfModule mod_headers.c>
  Header unset Etag
</IfModule>

FileETag None
```

Upload the `.htaccess` file to the folder to which you want the rules to apply.

How it works...

First, we unset ETag for those files that are currently configured:

```
<IfModule mod_headers.c>
  Header unset Etag
</IfModule>
```

Second, we use `FileTag None` to make sure files have ETags removed:

```
FileETag None
```

There's more...

The following section provides some more information about ETags for your reference.

Synchronizing ETag values on an IIS server

If you are running an IIS server, to resolve the problem, you must synchronize the ETag values on all the Web servers that are running IIS 5.0 in the Web farm. To do this, use the `Mdutil.exe` tool to retrieve the ETag value from one of the Web servers. Then, set the same ETag value on all the other Web servers.

More detailed instructions can be found in the following Microsoft Support article:

```
http://support.microsoft.com/?id=922733
```

High performance websites

Steve Souders has explained configuring rules in his *High Performance Web Sites* series:

High Performance Web Sites: Rule 13 – Configure ETags:

```
http://developer.yahoo.com/blogs/ydn/posts/2007/07/high_
performanc_11/
```

David Walsh blog

David Walsh's blog website contains a post by Eric Wendelin – *Improve Your YSlow Grade Using .htaccess* and this also mentions the issues addressed in this recipe:

```
http://davidwalsh.name/yslow-htaccess
```

MBP – Mobile Boilerplate

Entity tag removal is also included in the Mobile Boilerplate:

```
https://github.com/h5bp/mobile-boilerplate/blob/master/.
htaccess#L211-L218
```

9
Mobile Performance Testing

In this chapter, we will cover:

- ► Mobile testing your device with Blaze
- ► Analyzing mobile page speed online
- ► PCAP Web Performance Analyzer
- ► HTTP Archive Mobile
- ► Storing performance data with Jdrop

Introduction

In this chapter, we will go through some of the hottest mobile performance testing tools.

Like mobile debugging, mobile performance testing may not be as straightforward as desktop testing. But for every cloud, there is a silver lining. Many developers have found creative ways to address such issues.

Speed testing your device with Blaze

Target browsers: cross-browser

If you want to save time and quickly test the performance of a mobile site to know the load times and information about page resources, then Blaze is a good choice. The Mobitest Performance Tool is used to understand mobile web performance. It provides the following test results:

- ▸ Overall load times
- ▸ Breakdown of individual page resources
- ▸ Rendering video
- ▸ Raw HTTP Archive (HAR) file

Getting ready

All you have to do is to log on to `http://www.blaze.io/mobile/`.

How to do it...

On the page, you can see the following form that allows you to enter a URL. Let's put **yahoo. com** to the test!

At the top of the results page, we can see from the screenshot average load time, page size, and the speed ranking of the site:

The following diagram shows the waterfall chart of the site:

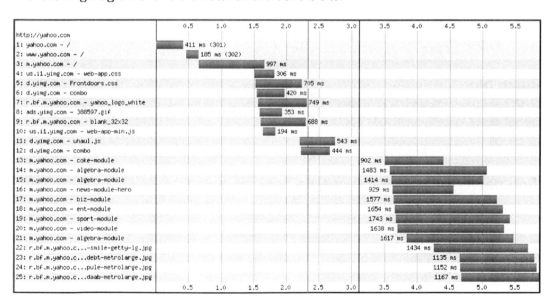

How it works...

Device used

You might be wondering what devices are used at the backend, and if they are emulators or simulators. The tests are run on real mobile devices using custom-built agents.

Load time percentile

An internal index is used to calculate the load time percentile. It uses hundreds of websites to get the speed of a site compared to other sites.

Location of the test run

The test run location is in Ottawa, Canada. The agents are connected to the Internet over WiFi. Devices used at the time of writing are: iPhone, Nexus, and Samsung Galaxy S.

To know more, visit:

```
http://www.blaze.io/mobile/methodology/.
```

There's more...

A list of useful page test tools can be found at:

```
http://www.blaze.io/learn/feo-resources/
```

Blaze blog

Apart from the testing tools provided, there is also a blog run by Blaze with great articles talking about everything mobile optimization-related at:

```
http://www.blaze.io/blog/
```

Web performance optimization best practices

For good tips about web performance best practices, visit the Blaze optimization page at:

```
http://www.blaze.io/overview/optimizations/
```

Analyzing mobile page speed online

Target browsers: cross-browser

If you are familiar with Google Page Speed, you know that there is a Chrome extension to test load time on desktop browsers. But there is also a web version of Google Page Speed that can be used to analyze mobile performance.

Getting ready

Visit Google Page Speed Online at:

```
http://pagespeed.googlelabs.com/.
```

How to do it...

In this example, we will test Google's mobile home page:

1. Enter a URL you want to analyze, in our case, let's use **m.google.com**:

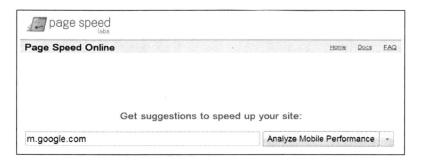

2. Click on the drop-down list next to the input box and choose **Get mobile suggestions** from the drop-down menu:

3. Once clicking on **Analyze Mobile Performance**, we reach a page that looks as follows:

Mobile page summary

The page Google Mobile got an overall Page Speed Score of **62** (out of 100). Learn more

> 💡 This Page Speed report is generated for this page as it appears on mobile devices. To get a Page Speed report for desktop clients, view the desktop report instead.

Details

Click on the rule names to see suggestions for improvement.

* **High priority**. These suggestions represent the largest potential performance wins for the least development effort. You should address this item first:
  Combine images into CSS sprites

* **Medium priority**. These suggestions may represent smaller wins or much more work to implement. However, there are no medium priority suggestions for this site. Good job!

* **Low priority**. These suggestions represent the smallest wins. You should only be concerned with these items after you've handled the higher-priority ones:
  Minimize redirects, Minify HTML

* **Experimental rules**. These suggestions are experimental, but do not affect the overall Page Speed score. Consider this item as a pointer to an area to explore, but your mileage might vary:
  Use an Application Cache

* **Rules without suggestions**. There are no suggestions for these rules, since this page already follows these best practices. Good job!

How it works...

The Page Speed Score indicates how much faster a page could be. For our example, the number is 62 out of 100.

The following are details of the analysis. The details have been broken down as follows:

* High priority: These suggestions represent the largest potential performance winners for the least development effort. You should address these items first.

* Medium priority: These suggestions may represent smaller wins or much more work to implement.

* Low priority: These suggestions represent the smallest wins.

* Experimental rules: These suggestions are experimental, but do not affect the overall Page Speed score.

* Rules without suggestions: There are no suggestions for these rules, as this page already follows these best practices. But you can still check the rules by expanding the collapsible menu on the left.

There's more...

To see a list of Mobile Performance Tools, visit:

```
https://github.com/h5bp/mobile-boilerplate/wiki/Mobile-Performance-
Tools
```

The need for speed

MIT technology review shows some charts and statistics about how important speed is and how it affects your site's visitors. The article mentions that even slight slowdowns online frustrate people and cost companies money:

```
http://www.technologyreview.com/files/54902/GoogleSpeed_charts.pdf
```

When seconds count

A national consumer survey on website and mobile performance expectations was conducted by Gomez Inc:

```
http://www.gomez.com/wp-content/downloads/GomezWebSpeedSurvey.pdf
```

Analyzing mobile performance with PCAP Web Performance Analyzer

Target browsers: cross-browser

PCAP Web Performance Analyzer allows you to have greater control over data analysis. You can interact with the mobile website/application and get the performance data more accurately. It's created by *Bryan McQuade* and *Libo Song*.

Getting ready

Before using PCAP Web Performance Analyzer, we need to first capture PCAP files for mobile devices. We do so by setting up a private WiFi network, connect the mobile device to the network, capture, and then analyze the traffic. Here is how to do it:

1. Open **Control Panel | Network and Internet | Network and Sharing Center**.
2. Select the link for **Set up a new connection or network**.
3. Select **Set up a wireless ad hoc (computer-to-computer) network**.
4. Next, give the network a name (hot1, for example), and check **Save this network**.
5. Go back to **Network and Sharing Center**, click on the **Change adapter settings** link on the left.

6. Find your LAN, right-click and open **Properties | Sharing tab**.

7. Enable sharing.

Now we have to download Wireshark which we can use to choose the network traffic that we want to capture. We can generate the HAR file and save it on the local machine using the following steps:

1. Download Wireshark from: `http://www.wireshark.org/download.html`.

2. Open WireShark.

3. Click on **Menu Capture | Options**.

4. In the **Options** dialog, select your wireless interface, and click on **Capture Filter**.

5. In the **Capture Filter** dialog, create a new filter (if you have not already done so), with the name **TCP and UDP port 53 (DNS)**, and filter string as **tcp or udp port 53**.

6. Select the filter, then close the dialog.

7. Click on the **Start** button in the **Capture Options** dialog to start capturing.

8. Save the capture when done.

To connect a mobile device to a hotspot, on your mobile device connect to the WiFi hotspot specified ("hot1" in our example). Now, any websites you visit on your mobile device should be captured by *tcpdump*.

How to do it...

On the **Performance Analyzer** page, select your saved HAR file and click on **Upload**. The file will be processed and a detailed analysis with Waterfall will be displayed:

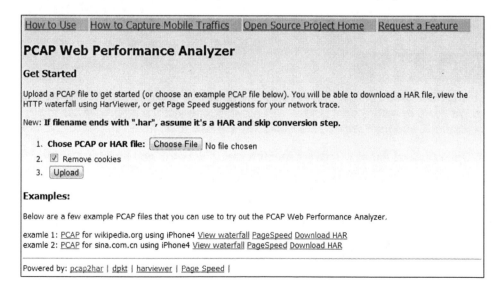

How to Use   How to Capture Mobile Traffics   Open Source Project Home   Request a Feature

PCAP Web Performance Analyzer

Get Started

Upload a PCAP file to get started (or choose an example PCAP file below). You will be able to download a HAR file, view the HTTP waterfall using HarViewer, or get Page Speed suggestions for your network trace.

New: If filename ends with ".har", assume it's a HAR and skip conversion step.

1. **Chose PCAP or HAR file:** [Choose File] No file chosen
2. ☑ Remove cookies
3. [Upload]

Examples:

Below are a few example PCAP files that you can use to try out the PCAP Web Performance Analyzer.

examle 1: PCAP for wikipedia.org using iPhone4 View waterfall PageSpeed Download HAR
examle 2: PCAP for sina.com.cn using iPhone4 View waterfall PageSpeed Download HAR

Powered by: pcap2har | dpkt | harviewer | Page Speed |

How it works...

It uses open file formats PCAP and HAR, and open source tools pcap2har, HAR viewer, and Page Speed.

There's more...

Stoyan Stefanov maintains a hugely useful site about web and mobile performance:

```
http://calendar.perfplanet.com/2010/mobile-performance-analysis-
using-pcapperf/
```

HAR viewer

As it says on the official description, *HAR Viewer is a web application (PHP + JavaScript) that allows visualizing HTTP tracing logs based on HTTP Archive format (HAR)*. The project is hosted on Google Code; you can check it out at: `http://code.google.com/p/harviewer/`.

Using Page Speed to optimize your website for mobile

There is a video on using Google's Page Speed. The video was shot during Google I/O 2011, presented by the creators of PACPPERF and can be found at:

```
http://www.google.com/events/io/2011/sessions/use-page-speed-to-
optimize-your-web-site-for-mobile.html
```

pcap2har

To know more about pcap2har, you can visit the project page hosted on Github at:

```
https://github.com/andrewf/pcap2har
```

Using HTTP Archive Mobile

Target browsers: cross-browser

HTTP Archive Mobile tracks how the Web is built. It provides:

- ▶ **Trends in web technology**: Load times, download sizes, performance scores
- ▶ **Interesting stats**: Popular scripts, image formats, errors, redirects
- ▶ **Website performance**: Specific URL screenshots, waterfall charts, HTTP headers

Getting ready

Log on to `http://mobile.httparchive.org/`.

How to do it...

Click on **Trends** and you can see the trends such as transfer size and requests of HTML, JavaScript, CSS, Image, and Flash. The following is the chart of HTML Transfer Size & HTML Requests:

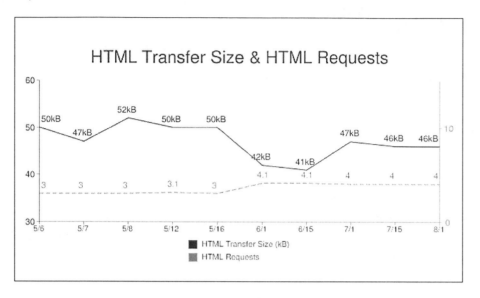

Click on **Stats** and you can get many interesting stats, from most common image formats to most common servers; from pages with the most CSS to pages with the most images.

The following is a chart showing the most popular JS libraries:

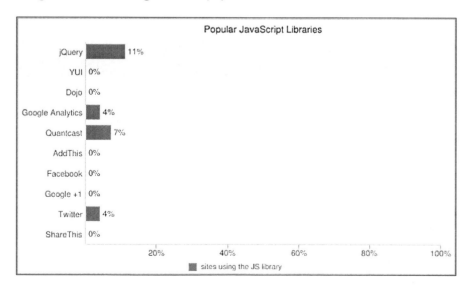

Click on **Websites** and you will get all the performance information relating to a particular site, including Filmstrip, Waterfall, Page speed, Requests, Trends, and Downloads of the HAR file.

How it works...

The sites listed are the ones that ranked top by Alexa, Fortune, Global 500, and Quancast10K.

The list of URLs is fed to WebPagetest.org.

The HTTP waterfall chart is generated from the HAR file using JavaScript.

There's more...

So, you may ask why we need to record the data. We do so because it is important to archive and learn from the history of web performance. As *Steve Souders* says, *'The HTTP Archive provides this record. It is a permanent repository of web performance information such as size of pages, failed requests, and technologies utilized.'* (at http://www.stevesouders. com/blog/2011/03/30/announcing-the-http-archive/).

How accurate is the data?

If you are wondering about the data accuracy, have a read at: http://mobile. httparchive.org/about.php#accuracy about the measurements, in particular the time measurements.

Limitation of the testing methodology

Although the test results are largely useful, there are limitations that users need to take note of. For a list of things to consider, visit:

http://mobile.httparchive.org/about.php#limitations

Storing performance data with Jdrop

Target browsers: cross-browser

Jdrop is used to store mobile device performance data. The JSON data are stored in the cloud.

Mobile device has small screen real estate, which makes analyzing huge chunks of information difficult. To counter the problem, Jdrop allows you to analyze data gathered from mobile devices on the large screen.

Getting ready

Sign in to Jdrop at `http://jdrop.org/`.

How to do it...

On your mobile device:

1. Sign in to Jdrop.
2. Install any of the apps that use Jdrop.
3. Run the app and save data to Jdrop.

On your desktop or laptop:

1. Sign in to Jdrop.
2. View the JSON data that you generated.

On mobile devices, the easiest way to start is to embed the contents of `jdrop-example.js` (can be found at: `http://jdrop.org/jdrop-example.js`) in your bookmarklet script. In addition, you also have to add a *Save to Jdrop* link to your bookmarklet that calls your function. You can find the code with explanation at: `http://jdrop.org/devdocs`.

Saving to Jdrop:

Here's the code you need to add a *Save to Jdrop* link to your bookmarklet.

```
<a href="javascript:SaveToJdrop('MY APP NAME', myDataObj, '1.1.3',
'1.8 secs')">Save to Jdrop</a>
```

Registering your app:

For now, registering your app requires a bit of manual work; you have to post a request to the Jdrop discussion list (`http://groups.google.com/group/jdrop/topics`).

This is the information needed to register your app:

- **App Name** (required)
- **Script URL** (required)
- **Callback Function** (optional)
- **Format** (optional)
- **Format Key** (optional)

Some of the information might be changed by the time you read this, and you can log on to `http://jdrop.org/devdocs` to check if there are any updates.

How it works...

You might be wondering why Jdrop asks for access to your Google Contacts when connecting through a Google account. This is because OAuth to Google requires mentioning a service to authenticate with. Jdrop doesn't actually access any of your contacts. The creators are looking at OpenID instead of OAuth as a way to bypass this step.

There's more...

Jdrop was created by *Steve Souders* and *James Pearce*.

Steve Souders is no stranger to most developers; to see all the wonders he has created, go to:

`http://stevesouders.com/`.

James Pearce is the director of developer relations at Sencha Inc. You can find interesting ideas and useful information about mobile on his website at:

`http://tripleodeon.com/`.

10
Emerging Mobile Web Features

In this chapter, we will cover:

- ▸ `window.onerror`
- ▸ Using ECMAScript 5 methods
- ▸ New HTML5 input types
- ▸ Inline SVG
- ▸ `position:fixed`
- ▸ `overflow:scroll`

Introduction

Mobile Safari on iOS 5 has introduced a series of improvements that makes mobile Safari one of the most advanced mobile browsers. A lot of cutting edge HTML5 features—ECMAScript 5 as well as mobile-specific features — were added to allow more functionality with mobile and boost the performance:

- ▸ **Web forms** has been introduced to help with a better user interface for the Web, making interface prototyping much quicker and easier.
- ▸ **Inline SVG** allows greater scalability on mobile browsers; this could be useful for responsive design.
- ▸ **ES5** allows greater control over the objects created, and large and complex features can be built in pure JavaScript.

> ▶ **Mobile-specific properties** such as scrolling CSS were added. On mobile Safari, it was once painful to achieve the native scrolling, but now mobile-specific properties have been added to make it pain free for web developers to develop web apps that have the same performance as native applications.

window.onerror

Target browsers: iOS 5

In iOS 5, there is a newly added event handler: `window.onerror`. This event handler is for error events sent to the window.

The syntax looks as follows:

```
window.onerror = funcA;
```

Getting ready

Create an HTML document and name it `ch10r01.html`.

How to do it...

Enter the following code and test it in the browser:

```html
<!doctype html>
<html>
  <head>
    <title>Mobile Cookbook</title>
    <meta charset="utf-8">
    <style>
    </style>
  </head>
  <body>
    <script>
    window.onerror=function(){
     alert('An error has occurred!')
    }
    </script>
    <script>
    document.write('hello world'
    </script>
  </body>
</html>
```

You should see a pop-up alert saying an error has occurred.

How it works...

The error occurred because we didn't close the bracket in `document.write`:

```
<script>
  document.write('hello world'
</script>
```

If you close the bracket and try again, the error will disappear:

```
<script>
  document.write('hello world');
</script>
```

There's more...

The default window behavior is to prevent error dialogs from displaying. It overwrites the default behavior:

```
window.onerror = null;
```

Browser Object Model

The **Browser Object Model (BOM)** is a collection of objects that give you access to the browser and the computer screen. These objects are accessible through the global objects window and `window.screen`. To find out more about BOM, visit:

```
http://javascript.about.com/od/browserobjectmodel/Browser_Object_
Model.htm
```

Using ECMAScript 5 methods

Target browsers: iOS 5

ECMAScript 5 is replacing ECMAScript 3.1. ECMAScript 5 provides a great enhancement to object interaction. Starting with iOS 4, Safari introduced many new ECMAScript 5 features; iOS 5 brought even greater support for ECMAScript 5.

The following are the newly introduced `Object` methods:

```
Object.seal/Object.isSealed
Object.freeze/Object.isFrozen
Object.preventExtensions/Object.isExtensible
Function.prototype.bind
```

Getting ready

Create an HTML document and name it ch10r02.html.

How to do it...

Enter the following code and test it in the browser:

```
/*** freeze ***/

var dog = {
  eat: function () {},
  hair: "black"
};
var o = Object.freeze(dog);

// test if dog is frozen
assert(Object.isFrozen(dog) === true);

// can't alter the property
dog.hair = "yellow";

// can't remove property
delete dog.hair;

// can't add new property
dog.height = "0.5m";

/*** seal ***/

var human = {
  eat: function () {},
  hair: "black"
};
human.hair = "blonde";
var o = Object.seal(obj);
// changing property works
human.hair = "grey";
// can't convert
Object.defineProperty(obj, "hair", { get: function() { return "green";
} });
// silently doesn't add the property
human.height = "1.80m";
// silently doesn't delete the property
```

```
delete human.hair;
// detect if an object is sealed
assert(Object.isSealed(human) === true);

/*** preventExtensions ***/

var nonExtensible = { removable: true };
Object.preventExtensions(nonExtensible);
Object.defineProperty(nonExtensible, "new", { value: 8675309 });
// throws a TypeError
assert(Object.isExtensible(nonExtensible) === true);

/*** bind ***/

var x = 9;
var module = {
  x: 81,
  getX: function() { return this.x; }
};

module.getX(); // 81

var getX = module.getX;
getX(); // 9, because in this case, "this" refers to the global object

// create a new function with 'this' bound to module
var boundGetX = getX.bind(module);
boundGetX(); // 81
```

How it works...

Freeze

As the name says, `freeze` freezes an object. Nothing can be added to or removed from `freeze`; you can't even alter the content. It makes an object immutable and returns a frozen object:

```
// can't alter the property
dog.hair = "yellow";

// can't remove property
delete dog.hair;

// can't add new property
dog.height = "0.5m";
```

To test if an object is frozen, use `isFrozen`:

```
// test if dog is frozen
assert(Object.isFrozen(dog) === true);

// silently doesn't add the property
human.height = "1.80m";

// silently doesn't delete the property
delete human.hair;
```

Seal

If you `seal` an object, the object properties can no longer be added or removed. You might ask, what is the difference between `freeze` and `seal`? The difference is that for `seal`, you can still change the value of the present properties:

```
// changing property works
human.hair = "grey";
```

To test if an object is sealed, use `isSealed`:

```
// detect if an object is sealed
assert(Object.isSealed(human) === true);
```

preventExtensions

By default, an object is extensible, but with `preventExtensions`, we can prevent an object from extending. This means no new properties can be further added to the object.

```
/*** preventExtensions ***/

var nonExtensible = { removable: true };
Object.preventExtensions(nonExtensible);
Object.defineProperty(nonExtensible, "new", { value: 8675309 });
// throws a TypeError
assert(Object.isExtensible(nonExtensible) === true);
```

Function.prototype.bind

Another extremely useful feature introduced is `bind`. It allows greater control of the `this` value. In our example, no matter how the function is called, it is called with a particular `this` value.

From the example, we can see there is a global variable x, and its value is modified in the `module` object:

```
var x = 9;
var module = {
  x: 81,
  getX: function() { return this.x; }
};

module.getX(); // 81
```

When extracting the method `getX` from the object, later call that function and expect it to use the original object as `this`, but at this time, the object is global, and so it returns 9.

```
var getX = module.getX;
getX(); // 9, because in this case, "this" refers to the global object
```

By using `bind`, we create a new function with `this` bound to `module`:

```
// create a new function with 'this' bound to module
var boundGetX = getX.bind(module);
boundGetX(); // 81
```

There's more...

The default window behavior is to prevent error dialogs from displaying. It overwrites the default behavior:

```
window.onerror = null;
```

Documentation on MDN

`Object.freeze/Object.isFrozen`:

- https://developer.mozilla.org/en/JavaScript/Reference/Global_Objects/Object/freeze
- https://developer.mozilla.org/en/JavaScript/Reference/Global_Objects/Object/isFrozen

`Object.seal/Object.isSealed`:

- https://developer.mozilla.org/en/JavaScript/Reference/Global_Objects/Object/seal
- https://developer.mozilla.org/en/JavaScript/Reference/Global_Objects/Object/isSealed

preventExtensions/isExtensible:

- ▶ https://developer.mozilla.org/en/JavaScript/Reference/
  Global_Objects/Object/preventExtensions
- ▶ https://developer.mozilla.org/en/JavaScript/Reference/
  Global_Objects/Object/isExtensible

Function.prototype.bind:

- ▶ https://developer.mozilla.org/en/JavaScript/Reference/
  Global_Objects/Function/bind

New HTML5 input types

Target browsers: iOS 5

New input types are useful features for web forms. iOS 5 now supports: date, datetime, month, time, range, and more.

Getting ready

Create an HTML document and name it ch10r03.html.

How to do it...

Enter the following code and test it in the browser:

```html
<!doctype html>
<html>
  <head>
    <title>Mobile Cookbook</title>
    <meta charset="utf-8">

  </head>
  <body>
    <input type="date">
    <input type="datetime">
    <input type="month">
    <input type="time">
    <input type="range">
  </body>
</html>
```

How it works...

On iOS 5, date and datetime will be rendered as follows:

Once rendered on iOS Safari, the month and time input type will look like the following screenshot:

The `slider` input type will look like the following screenshot:

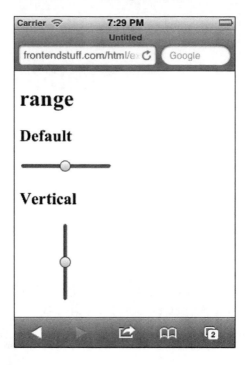

There's more...

There are many polyfills used to make web forms work cross browser. `html5slider` is a JavaScript implementation of HTML5 `<input type="range">` for Firefox 4 and above. You can learn more about it at:

`https://github.com/fryn/html5slider`

Inline SVG in text/HTML

Target browsers: iOS 5

Scalable Vector Graphics (**SVG**) can be used in an HTML document with the support of inline SVG.

Getting ready

Create an HTML document and name it `ch10r04.html`.

How to do it...

Enter the following code and test it in the browser:

```
<svg width="500" height="220" xmlns="http://www.w3.org/2000/svg"
version="1.1">
  <rect x="2" y="2" width="496" height="216" stroke="#000"
stroke-width="2px" fill="transparent"></rect>
</svg>
```

How it works...

HTML inline SVG has to be rendered with a MIME type `Content-Type: text/xml`. You can create this by ending the document with `.xml` instead of `.html`.

There's more...

There are several ways to embed SVG in HTML pages: `<object>`, `<embed>`, `<iframe>`.

To find out more about SVG support in different browsers, visit (under section *Embed SVG code directly into the HTML*):

`http://www.w3schools.com/svg/svg_inhtml.asp`

SVG in HTML

Mozilla MDN has a lot of useful articles about frontend web and related information:

`https://developer.mozilla.org/en/SVG_In_HTML_Introduction`

position:fixed

Target browsers: iOS 5

`position:fixed` is now supported in iOS 5. It's now much easier to create fixed positioned toolbars for web apps.

Getting ready

Create an HTML document and name it `ch10r05.html`.

How to do it...

Before iOS 5, `position:fixed` didn't work in mobile Safari. If we wanted to create a toolbar or a fixed positioned header or footer, something like the following hack was needed:

```
<div id="fixedDiv">
</div>
<script>
window.onscroll = function() {
  document.getElementById('fixedDiv').style.top =
      (window.pageYOffset + window.innerHeight - 25) + 'px';
};
</script>
```

With the release of iOS 5, the hack is no longer needed, we could simply use CSS style the way we normally use it for other browsers:

```
<style>
  #fixedDiv { position:fixed; }
</style>
<div id="fixedDiv">
</div>
```

How it works...

We register the `onscroll` event to the `window` object, when the scrolling event happens, the `div` will always be at the bottom of the page.

```
https://developer.mozilla.org/en/SVG_In_HTML_Introduction
```

overflow:scroll

Target browsers: iOS 5

One big difference between mobile and desktop is the way people interact with the browser. If you have a scrolling action on the desktop browser, it can be done by a mouse wheel or a scrollbar. On mobile browser, there isn't a scrollbar or a mouse wheel, so the entire scroll interaction is done by finger action. For a long time, `overflow:scroll` wasn't supported by iOS, but now it's supported by iOS 5!

Getting ready

Create an HTML document and name it `ch10r06.html`.

How to do it...

Now if you want to make an area scrollable, use the following code:

```html
<!doctype html>
<html>
  <head>
    <title>Mobile Cookbook</title>
    <meta charset="utf-8">
    <meta name="viewport" content="width=device-width,
initial-scale=1.0">
    <style>
      div {
        width:200px;
        height:200px;
        margin:0 auto;
        border:1px solid black;
        overflow: scroll;
        -webkit-overflow-scrolling: touch;
      }
    </style>
  </head>
  <body>
  <div>
    <p>Lorem Ipsum</p>
    <p>Lorem Ipsum</p>
    <p>Lorem Ipsum</p>
    <p>Lorem Ipsum</p>
    <p>Lorem Ipsum</p>
    <p>Lorem Ipsum</p>
    <p>Lorem Ipsum</p>
    <p>Lorem Ipsum</p>
    <p>Lorem Ipsum</p>
    <p>Lorem Ipsum</p>
    <p>Lorem Ipsum</p>
    <p>Lorem Ipsum</p>
    <p>Lorem Ipsum</p>
    <p>Lorem Ipsum</p>
     <p>Lorem Ipsum</p>
  </div>
  </body>
</html>
```

How it works...

By defining `overflow` as `scroll` and `-webkit-overflow-scrolling` as `touch`, one can scroll content on a mobile Safari page without any additional code.

There's more...

In the past few years, there have been many hacks used to fake the native scroll behavior. The never-released web framework **PastryKit** by Apple inspired many frameworks to do this. Some notable ones are:

- Sencha touch: `http://www.sencha.com/products/touch/`
- iScroll: `http://cubiq.org/iscroll`
- Scrollability: `https://github.com/joehewitt/scrollability/`
- jQuery mobile: `http://jquerymobile.com/`

There is an old saying *"Fake it till you make it"*. And now Apple has finally made it possible to do so natively. And performance-wise, it's pretty solid and could perform better than any previous frameworks.

Browser fragmentation

For certain businesses, there might be the concern of fragmentation of mobile browsers. One approach is to support browsers two versions before the current browser version. Also, another approach is to use the user market share as a cut-off point.

Index

G

gamma property 134
geolocation
    geolocation map based, building 121-125
    map based geolocation, building 124
    using, with foursquare 134, 136
geo-location-javascript 119
geo_position_js.init() 121
gesturechange event 83
gestureend event 83
GestureEvent class
    on Safari, URL 83
gesture events
    and Google Maps 84
    image, zooming with 82, 83
    used, for rotating HTML element 74-76
gesturestart event 83
getCurrentPosition method 118
getX method 221
Google
    and mobile-friendly site, building 114
    and mobile site, indexing 114
Google Analytics
    accuracy 9
    alternatives 9
    URL 7
Google Code blog 147
Google Maps JavaScript API V3
    URL 125
Gzip
    used, for compressing files 194-196

H

home screen button icon
    adding 36, 37
    Apple custom Icon 39
    Apple touch icons 39
    Image creation guidelines 39
    starting with 36
    target devices 36
    touch icons 39
    working 37, 38
HTML
    and mobile web, processing 5, 6

HTML5
    and version number 19
    CSS reset 22
    elements 22
    on mobile web 18, 19
    rendering, across different browsers 20, 22
    resources, URL 19
HTML5 Doctor
    URL 19
HTML5 draft
    W3C 19
    WHATWG 19
HTML5 Rocks
    about 147
    URL 19
HTML5 semantics
    used, for building pages 86-88
html5shim 22
html5slider
    URL 224
HTML5 specs
    W3C version, URL 20
HTML5 storage wars 152
HTML document
    creating 116
HTML element
    rotating, with gesture events 74-76
HTTP Archive Mobile
    testing methodology, limitations 211
    using 209
    using, steps 210, 211

I

IIS server
    ETag values, synchronizing 198
Inline SVG 215
innerShiv 22
input types, HTML5
    about 222
    date 223
    datetime 223
    slider 224
instant response
    used, for making buttons 106-108
interval property 133

scale bug fix
   drawback 77
Scrollability
   URL 228
seal 220
Sencha touch
   URL 228
server-side
   processing 9
session API
   Flash-like navigation, creating 157-161
showInfo function 118
simulator
   browser 11
   community-based collection, URL 17
   device 10, 11
   Firtman collection, URL 17
slider input type 224
Smartphone frontend Matrices
   URL 33
stable channel 173
SVG
   about 224
   browser support, URL 225
   code, testing 225
   HTML inline SVG 225
   in HTML 225
swipe events
   about 77, 80
   and Zepto framework 81
Swipe Left Gesture
   URL 81

T

target mobile devices
   identifying 6, 7
text resize
   about 39
   issue, solving 42
   preventing 40-42
   px vs em 43
   Windows Mobile 43
text-size-adjust 42
this value 220

touchend event 83
touch events
   used, for moving element 63-65
touchmove event 65
touchstart event 83

U

Ultimate CSS Gradient Generator 93
user agent detection
   applying 100-102

V

video
   streaming, on mobile 142-144
viewport width
   about 44
   Blackberry documentation 47
   IE, for Windows Phone viewport blog post 47
   optimizing 44-46
   Safari documentation 47
   working 46

W

W3C 19
W3C Audio Working Group
   URL 141
web forms 215
WebKit chrome
   hiding 109-112
WebKit features
   disabling 59-61
   limiting 59-61
   narrow screen ellipsis 62
   tap color, changing 62
   textarea content 62
   working 62
webkit-overflow-scrolling 228
web storage
   portability layer 151
   using, on mobile 148-151
web workers
   using 152-156

Thank you for buying
HTML5 Mobile Development Cookbook

About Packt Publishing

Packt, pronounced 'packed', published its first book "*Mastering phpMyAdmin for Effective MySQL Management*" in April 2004 and subsequently continued to specialize in publishing highly focused books on specific technologies and solutions.

Our books and publications share the experiences of your fellow IT professionals in adapting and customizing today's systems, applications, and frameworks. Our solution based books give you the knowledge and power to customize the software and technologies you're using to get the job done. Packt books are more specific and less general than the IT books you have seen in the past. Our unique business model allows us to bring you more focused information, giving you more of what you need to know, and less of what you don't.

Packt is a modern, yet unique publishing company, which focuses on producing quality, cutting-edge books for communities of developers, administrators, and newbies alike. For more information, please visit our website: www.packtpub.com.

Writing for Packt

We welcome all inquiries from people who are interested in authoring. Book proposals should be sent to author@packtpub.com. If your book idea is still at an early stage and you would like to discuss it first before writing a formal book proposal, contact us; one of our commissioning editors will get in touch with you.

We're not just looking for published authors; if you have strong technical skills but no writing experience, our experienced editors can help you develop a writing career, or simply get some additional reward for your expertise.

PhoneGap Beginner's Guide

ISBN: 978-1-84951-536-8   Paperback: 320 pages

Enhance your JSF web applications using powerful AJAX components

1. Learn how to use the PhoneGap mobile application framework

2. Develop cross-platform code for iOS, Android, BlackBerry, and more

3. Write robust and extensible JavaScript code

4. Master new HTML5 and CSS3 APIs

Dreamweaver CS5.5 Mobile and Web Development with HTML5, CSS3, and jQuery

ISBN: 978-1-84969-158-1   Paperback: 284 pages

Harness the cutting edge features of Dreamweaver for mobile and web development

1. Create web pages in Dreamweaver using the latest technology and approach

2. Add multimedia and interactivity to your websites

3. Optimize your websites for a wide range of platforms and build mobile apps with Dreamweaver

4. A practical guide filled with many examples for making the best use of Dreamweaver's latest features

Please check **www.PacktPub.com** for information on our titles

jQuery Mobile First Look

ISBN: 978-1-84951-590-0   Paperback: 216 pages

Discover the endless possibilities offered by jQuery Mobile for rapid Mobile Web Development

1. Easily create your mobile web applications from scratch with jQuery Mobile

2. Learn the important elements of the framework and mobile web development best practices

3. Customize elements and widgets to match your desired style

4. Step-by-step instructions on how to use jQuery Mobile

Sencha Touch Cookbook

ISBN: 978-1-84951-544-3   Paperback: 328 pages

Over 100 recipes for creating cross platform rich media HTML5 apps

1. Master cross platform application development

2. Incorporate geo location into your apps

3. Develop native looking web apps

Please check **www.PacktPub.com** for information on our titles